Volcanic Kitchens

Come and join us

Photography by Gerhard Egger

Spring 8 Summe

Contents

Foreword

Before settling in Rotorua, we travelled extensively around the world. We were always interested in not only the landscape, but also the different cultures, the foods people ate, and the traditions that surrounded the way food was cooked and enjoyed.

This photographic recipe book is all about the area of New Zealand's Volcanic Plateau, first settled by the Te Arawa people. The region now enjoys a very international community and we have strived throughout this book to celebrate the diversity of the community we live in and the beautiful landscape that we enjoy.

The initial concept was to have representation from the community through recipes. Getting those recipes proved to be one of the hardest parts of putting the book together! A lot of people didn't feel 'their' recipes would be good enough and felt that they didn't have anything worthy to contribute—others just ran out of time to send us something. Consequently, we have filled in gaps with recipes that we have collected ourselves. Our recipes come from the classical ones that Gerhard learnt as chef and others that we have collected over the years. The book also includes some recipes from when we had a dessert and cake business in Auckland. All our recipes have been tested, and we trust we have transcribed those that we were given accurately.

What we wished to achieve was a book that showcased the environment we live in. A percentage of the money raised through the sale of the book will go to the local community.

Our thanks go to all those that sent in their contributions, thank you to those who didn't know us, but let us into their kitchens to be photographed. Friends and family who lent us their homes for styling the food shoots, and other friends who have helped with editing and layout advice.

So, make a cuppa, get out the book, and let the recipes inspire you to open your kitchen cupboards—now it's time to get cooking and have fun! After you have enjoyed your fantastic meal, go for a walk and smell the roses or redwoods, take the time to look around you and enjoy all the positives our Volcanic Plateau has to offer.

As Rotorua residents, this book means a lot to us and we hope you will also be able to identify with it.

Gerhard and Henri (Henrietta) Egger

The Taupo Volcanic Zone

Boiling mud, warm streams, pools of hot water, shooting geysers, and let's not forget that smell of rotten eggs—sulphur. Rotorua is in the centre of New Zealand's Taupo Volcanic Zone, also known as the Volcanic Plateau. This zone spreads from White Island, a still active marine volcano 43 km's off the coast of Whakatane, to the mountains of the Tongariro National Park: Mt Ngarahoe, Mt Ruapehu and Mt Tongario. This area was first settled by the people of Te Arawa when they arrived by waka on Aoteraroa's eastern shores. The Te Arawa people moved inland and settled mainly in the area around the Rotorua lakes. They refer to this entire territory as 'Mai Maketū ki Tongariro ... Ko Te Arawa te waka', which places the prow of the Te Arawa waka at Maketū on the Bay of Plenty coast, and the stern at Mt Tongariro.

The city of Rotorua sits on the western bank of Lake Rotorua, nestled between Mt Ngongotaha and Mt Tarawera. The lake is the largest of the 16 lakes around the Rotorua area, and is the crater lake of one of several large volcanoes in the Rotorua region. Around 200,000 years ago after a massive eruption, (or several eruptions), the underlying magma chamber collapsed creating a circular caldera which in turn, filled with water creating what we now know as Lake Rotorua, the second largest lake in the North Island.

In the centre of the lake is the well known Mokoia Island, formerly known as Te-Motu-tapu-a-Tinirau. Privately owned, the island is sacred to the people of Te Arawa. Mokoia is now a wild life sanctuary for many threatened species including the tieke (saddleback) and toutouwai (North Island robin). For the locals however, Mokoia is best known for the love story between a high ranking Maori Chief's daughter, Hinemoa, and her love, Tutanekai, a young warrior of lowly birth.

Geo—earth and therme—heat. There are around 1200 geothermal features in and around Rotorua. These include geysers, hot springs, mud pools, fumaroles and silica terraces. Pohutu Geyser at Whakarewarewa is New Zealand's largest geyser and erupts several times a day, shooting water up to 30 metres into the sky. Kuirau Park, in the centre of the city, provides easily accessible evidence of Rotorua's volcanic history. Here, clouds of steam drift across local roads, mud bubbles, pools of water boil and steam escapes from fumaroles. It is popular for both locals and tourists to sit and soak their feet in the public footbaths situated within the park.

South-east of Rotorua lies Mt Tarawera. The eruption of Mt Tarawera in 1886 destroyed much of the surrounding area, killing over 100 people, burying the village of Te Wairoa and the famous Pink and White Terraces. The eruption effectively split the mountain into two and created a 17km long fissure.

Mt Ngongotaha is north-west of the city, the summit of which is part of the Mt Ngongotaha Scenic Reserve.

The geothermal areas around Rotorua have cultural significance. Local Maori have, for centuries, used the steam and boiling water for cooking and washing. This is still practised today with food on the local marae being cooked in steam boxes, an easy way of cooking for large numbers of people.

Lake Taupo, an hour's drive south, is New Zealand's largest lake and also the result of a huge eruption some 27,000 years ago. The beautiful volcanoes at the southern end, covered in snow in winter, are still active with Mt Ruapehu last erupting in the winters of 1995 and 1996. In 1887 these three mountains, were part of 6,518 acres gifted to the Crown by the paramount chief of Ngāti Tūwharetoa, Horonuku (Te Heuheu Tūkino IV), thus ensuring their protection as part of the Tongario National Park, the first National Park in New Zealand and fourth in the world.

For those of us who are fortunate to live in this fascinating region the volcanic history of the area has created a great playground for us all to enjoy. Numerous lakes for swimming, boating and fishing, mountains for tramping and skiing, rivers for white water rafting, forest tracks for mountain biking and hot pools to soak in on a cold winters day, all on our door step — we are the lucky ones!

Spring Food

Asparagus Risotto

Serves 4 mains or 8 entrees

1 small onion
1 clove garlic
500g short grain rice
100ml sauvignon blanc wine
1½ ltr chicken or
vegetable stock
2 bunches of asparagus
1 lemon
70g butter
50g parmesan cheese
salt and pepper
lemon-infused olive oil

In a saucepan, sauté over a low heat the finely diced onion and garlic in half the butter until the onion is transparent. Add the rice and stir. Add the wine and half the stock, stir. Keep stirring. Place a lid on the saucepan and simmer for approximately 18–20 minutes, stirring occasionally. Add more liquid from the remaining stock when required.

While the risotto is cooking, cut the top quarter off the asparagus. Cut the spear tips in half lengthways, dip quickly into boiling water, remove and chill in iced water. Cut the remaining asparagus into small pieces, removing any stalky bits from the ends. Blanch for 2–3 minutes in boiling water, remove and chill in iced water. Process the small stalk pieces in a food processor until smooth (add a little liquid if required), and add finely grated lemon rind.

When the rice is cooked to al dente stage, stir in the asparagus puree, half the parmesan—grated, and the remaining butter. Adjust the seasoning and liquid so that the risotto is of a creamy consistency. Serve immediately in individual bowls. Garnish with the asparagus tips and shavings of parmesan cheese and drizzle with lemon-infused oil.

Spinach and Parmesan Muffins

¼ ltr milk
60ml sunflower oil
100g cheddar cheese
80g parmesan cheese
140g spinach
2 tsp chilli sauce
3 eggs
500g flour
3 tsp baking powder
¼ tsp salt
sesame seeds
pumpkin seeds

In a large bowl, place milk, oil, grated cheeses, finely chopped spinach, chilli sauce and lightly beaten eggs. Mix well. In a separate bowl sieve together the flour, baking powder and salt. Add the flour to the spinach mix and fold together until just combined.

Fill muffin moulds and bake at 180˚C for 20–25 minutes.

Chilled Avocado Soup

Serves 4-6

2 tbsp avocado oil
½ onion
2 cloves garlic
2 medium potatoes
500ml chicken stock
1 lime
2 large avocados
100ml cream
salt
cayenne pepper
20g shrimps
lemon-infused oil
mint leaves

Sweat the onions and garlic in avocado oil in a saucepan. Add the peeled and cubed potatoes, chicken stock and lime zest. Boil until very soft. While still warm, process in a food processor until smooth. Chill.

Just before serving, process the avocados with the lime juice in the food processor until smooth. Add the chilled potato base and then the cream, process to combine and season to taste.

Serve in a chilled bowl, garnish with shrimps and drizzle with lemon-infused oil and mint leaves.

Kahawai

Chris Prenner

The humble kahawai (Arripis trutta) is severely underrated. Kahawai are found all around New Zealand, and are relatively easy to catch from shore with rods or nets (no boat needed). They are a great source of protein and taste delicious. The firm flesh is ideal for stir fries, casseroles and soups.

Chris's Camping Kahawai Stew

Kahawai is a great addition to any seafood soup or casserole like bouillabaisse or Asian laksa. This recipe is great when camping at the beach.

2 x 420g cans chilli beans
2 onions
1 rib celery
2 courgettes
1 kg kahawai fillets

In a large pot sauté the onions and add chilli beans, diced celery and courgettes. Dice the kahawai fillets and add, cook slowly until the fish is just cooked. Serve with boiled spuds and wash down with a couple of cans of cold beer. If there are any mussels on the rocks—chuck them in as well.

Note of caution: ensure your tent is well ventilated!

Simple Kahawai Stir Fry

kahawai fillets
lemon juice
soy sauce
sweet chilli sauce
garlic
onion
vegetables of your choice,
fresh or frozen
cornflour
oil
Optional; oyster sauce, sesame oil,
asian style sauces
rice vermicelli or egg noodles

Cut fish fillets in half along the middle—if you wish, cut off the dark meat now—and cut into finger thick strips. Marinate the fish in lemon juice and sauces, and let rest. Cut your vegetables: carrot, courgette and capsicum are great, onion and garlic in slices. Preheat a frying pan, or even better a wok, dip the fish pieces in cornflour and seal them in the hot pan in a little oil. When half cooked, remove from the pan and add the vegetables. Cook the vegetables for 3 minutes, add the fish and be careful not to overcook. For a nice finish, add freshly chopped herbs and any of the optional sauces for flavour.
Serve with noodles either added to the pan and mixed together, or serve on a bed of noodles.
If someone in your family doesn't like fish, just tell them it is "Chicken Stir Fry". They will not know the difference. To this day it is my children's favourite chicken dish – psst... don't tell them!

Creamed Garlic Mussels

3 tbsp oil
2 kg green lipped mussels
5 cloves garlic
300ml cream
1 egg yolk
juice of 1 lemon
chopped parsley

Heat the oil in a heavy-based saucepan until smoking hot. Add cleaned, washed mussels and chopped garlic. Place a lid on the pan to steam the mussels open—this takes approximately 4–5 minutes, shaking occasionally. Once the mussels have opened, remove from the heat and strain the liquid into a separate saucepan. Add lemon juice to the strained liquid and bring to the boil. Lightly whisk together the egg yolk and cream and add to the mussel stock, heat to thicken but do not allow to boil.

Pour sauce over the mussels and serve immediately, sprinkled with chopped parsley.

Coconut Prawns with Mango and Lime Salsa

Serves 6 for an entrée

30 king prawns
1 lime
1 egg
2 tbsp cornflour
1 cup desiccated coconut
oil for frying

Salsa:
1 ripe mango
2 limes
1 red chilli
mint

Marinate the raw prawns, peeled with tail on, in lime juice for half an hour. Dip into cornflour, and then egg wash, coat with coconut. Deep fry the prawns quickly in hot oil.

Serve the prawns hot with the salsa and a side dish of rice.

Peel the mango and cut into small cubes. Peel the limes, cut out the segments, and squeeze out the juice from the leftover fruit. De-seed and finely chop the chilli and the mint. Mix all the ingredients together.

LAKE
TARAWERA

Central Basin

MOUNT TARAWERA

Hamill's Killer

Yallow Rabbit

Jack Sprall

Bleeding Smelt

Doll Fly

Booby Fly

Rainbow Trout

Smelt

Creole Blackened Trout

whole fresh trout
creole fish seasoning mix
whole lemon
bunch of parsley
flour
oil

Using a whole fish, scour the skin and season liberally with Creole Fish Seasoning Mix (see recipe below). Stuff the inside of the trout with fresh parsley and lemon cut into wedges. Dust with flour, and quickly brown both sides in a very hot pan in oil. Bake in the oven at 180°C for 20–30 minutes, depending on the size of the trout.

Creole Fish Seasoning Mix

3 tbsp salt
3 tbsp sweet paprika
2 tbsp white pepper
2 tbsp onion powder
2 tbsp garlic powder
¼ tsp cayenne pepper
¼ tsp ground black pepper

Mix together.

*"Good things come
to those who bait"*
Anonymous

Smoked Fish

Chris Prenner

The best fish for smoking are the ones with fat in the flesh: such as trout, kahawai, mackerel. The two most important ingredients for smoking fish are smoke and salt. I prefer to use rock salt as it has more flavour.

10g rock salt per kilo of fish
10g brown sugar per kilo of fish

Optional:
garlic
thyme
turmeric
cracked pepper
lemon juice
lemon zest
soy sauce
sweet chilli sauce
Worcester sauce

Split the fish in half along the backbone. You can cut the backbone and belly bones out; however, they are very easy to remove when the fish is cooked. Smaller fish can be left whole. Sprinkle the salt and sugar mix (and any of the additional flavours you wish to add) liberally over the trout and leave for about 12 hours in a refrigerator. You can hang the fish in the smoker or lay it, skin down, on a rack. If you are going to lay it flat on the rack you can also fill the belly cavity with different herbs.

For smoking, I light a fire first in the base of an old drum or fridge and let it burn down to a smoulder before I add the fish. You can use most hard woods for smoking, manuka, pohutukawa, most fruit trees, oak and European beech are good. For extra flavour add rosemary, juniper twigs or grape vine. Depending on the heat and the density of the smoke and the thickness of the fish, the smoking process can take from half an hour to several hours. The fish is usually cooked when it shows white protein flakes on the surface. You may continue smoking on a very low heat (cold smoke), to add some more flavour.

Chocolate Muffins

Carla Porter

These muffins are not only yummy, but when baked in small muffin tins they make an excellent addition to the school lunch box.

2 cups flour
4 tbsp cocoa
4 tsp baking powder
⅔ cup oil
½ tsp salt
1 cup sugar
2 eggs, beaten
1½ cups milk

Cream cheese mix:
150g soft cream cheese
2 tbsp sugar

Sift the dry ingredients. Add the remaining ingredients and mix well. Put a spoonful of muffin mixture into buttered muffin tins. Add cream cheese mix or a piece of chocolate and cover with another spoon of muffin mix.

Bake at 150°C for 15–18 minutes. Sprinkle with icing sugar.

Blend together.

The Spongy Pud

Isla Edward

I received this recipe from a nursing friend in Hamilton, Mrs Knight, she died about 40 years ago. The Spongy Pud has always been very popular with the Edward family. I have found it easy to prepare and not too sweet. I make a double quantity for the family.

2 tbsp butter or dripping
1 cup boiling water
½ cup of sugar
1 heaped cup flour
1 heaped cup raisins
1 tbsp baking powder

Dissolve the butter in hot water, then add sugar, fruit and baking powder, stir. Add the flour and stir to combine. Put into a greased basin and cover well with aluminium foil to ensure no water can get in. Stand the bowl in a saucepan, fill to halfway up the bowl with boiling water and cover. Simmer for 3–4 hours.

Serve with custard.

Quintessential love is a young owner with their pet on pet day!

Chocolate Cake

Judy Gregor

This recipe was obtained from a Cruising World magazine in the late 70's. Its introduction read, 'when you are nearing the end of a voyage and you want to celebrate but there is very little left in the store cupboard you probably have these ingredients for a chocolate cake'. I have made this recipe a thousand times—it is not glamorous but continues to be the favourite birthday cake.

1½ cups flour
1 cup sugar
1 tsp salt
1 tsp baking soda
3 tbsp cocoa
1 tsp vanilla
½ cup oil
1 tbsp malt vinegar
1 cup water

Sift together flour, sugar, salt, baking soda and cocoa.
Make 3 holes in the mixture and put in vanilla, oil and vinegar.
Pour over water and mix well.

Pour into 20cm lined cake tin and bake at 160˚C for 35 minutes.

Allow to cool in tin.

ROTORUA
DISTRICT
GROUP DAY

FOURTH

Sponsored By
PIAKO TRACTOR

Spring is a new beginning......
Anonymous

Hazel's Best Ever Shortbread

Beverley Harris

My late mother, Hazel Harris, passed this on to me and I make it every Christmas to give to friends.

225g butter
¾ cup icing sugar
1¼ cups flour
¾ cup cornflour

Cream together the butter and icing sugar. Sieve three times the flour and cornflour (don't know why but just do it anyway —Mum's words) then gradually add to the creamed butter and sugar. Chill in the fridge and then roll out. Cut into shapes, prick with a fork and bake at 160°C for 30 minutes.

Anzac Biscuits

Makes 10 large biscuits

125g flour
150g white sugar
100g desiccated coconut
115g rolled oats
100g butter
1 tbsp golden syrup
½ tsp bicarbonate soda
25ml boiling water

Mix together all the dry ingredients. Melt butter and golden syrup. Dissolve baking soda in water and add to the butter mix. Fold in the dry ingredients.

Put spoonfuls onto a greased baking tray and bake in a preheated oven at 170°C for 15–20 minutes.

Lemon Posset Pudding

Carla Porter

600ml cream
⅔ cup sugar
100ml lemon juice

Boil the cream and sugar, stirring for 3 minutes to reduce. Remove from the heat, stir in lemon juice. Pour into 6 martini glasses or ramekins. Refrigerate for at least 4 hours. Serve with fresh berries or honey wafers.

Elderberry Fritters

100g flour
2 eggs
40g sugar
salt
1 cup milk
elderberry flowers
oil for frying

Cut the elderberry flowers from the shrub, leaving a stem of 2–3cm, rinse carefully and leave to dry on a paper towel. Put flour, egg yolks, salt, and milk into a large bowl, and mix to a smooth batter consistency. Whisk the egg white with the sugar until stiff and fold into the batter mix. In a deep pan heat the oil to 180˚C. Holding the flowers by their stems lightly dip into the batter and deep fry in hot oil, once the batter has set, cut off the long stems with scissors before turning over. Once golden, remove from pan and rest on a paper towel to soak any excess oil.

Lightly sprinkle with icing sugar and serve with a fresh fruit coulis.

Note; if serving adults you can make a lighter batter by replacing the milk with white wine.

Classic Citron Tart

This dessert has a very delicate flavour. It is best when made with a homemade buttery sweet pastry rather than a bought one. Fresh and clean on your palette, it can be served with fresh fruit or berries, a coulis, or just by itself with a dollop of cream.

Pastry:
100g salted butter
200g high grade flour
60g castor sugar
1 egg
1 tsp vanilla

Filling:
200ml cream
120ml fresh lemon juice
6 eggs
250g castor sugar

Grate the chilled butter coarsely, add the rest of the ingredients and knead quickly into a pastry. You need to be quick, so that the pastry doesn't get too warm. Wrap in plastic and refrigerate for 30 minutes.

Roll out the pastry to 3.5–4mm thick and line a greased, floured 30cm flan tin, one with a removable bottom is best. Blind bake at 180°C for approximately 10 minutes until the pastry is very slightly coloured. Remove from the oven and reduce the temperature to 130°C.

Whisk lightly together the citron filling ingredients, and strain through a sieve. Fill the pastry shell with the citron mix and bake for 40 minutes.

"For every chocoholic there is a budding lemonphile.."

Anonymous

Lemon and Almond Biscuits

1 cup flour
¼ tsp salt
1 cup blanched almonds
¾ cup raw sugar
½ cup treacle
110g butter
2 lemons

In a large bowl, combine the sifted flour and salt with the finely chopped almonds. Put the sugar, treacle, and butter in a saucepan and bring to the boil. Remove from the heat and fold in the flour mixture. Add the finely grated zest from the two lemons and 1 tablespoon of lemon juice. Mix to a smooth batter.

Lightly grease two baking trays. Place small spoonfuls of the batter onto the trays, approximately half a teaspoon, and bake separately for 8–10 minutes, or until a very light brown, at 180°C.

Allow to cool slightly before removing from the tray.

Amaretto Parfait

This recipe is with Amaretto but you can use any liqueur, the recipe works well Grand Marnier or Cointreau. Parfait is very simple to make and can be made and frozen a few days in advance, serve with fresh berries.

3 eggs
3 egg yolks
150g castor sugar
pinch of salt
1 tbsp vanilla essence
½ cup Amaretto
½ ltr cream

Place all the ingredients, other than the cream, in a mixing bowl and constantly whisk over steam until the mixture is warm.
Once warm, remove from the steam and whisk further until thick.
Whip the cream and fold in a third to the egg mix, then fold in the remaining cream. Pour into a container and freeze.

Best served with fresh strawberries.

"Food is our common ground, a universal experience"
James Beard

Chocolate Mousse

Geoffrey Hewlett

4–6 Servings

150g cooking chocolate, 70% cacao
4 eggs
300ml cream
4 tbsp sugar
pinch of salt

Break chocolate into the top of a double boiler. Melt slowly over warm water, DO NOT overheat. Whisk together the eggs, sugar and salt over steam until warm. Remove from heat and continue to whisk until thick and creamy. Add one third of egg mixture to chocolate and mix well. Add the chocolate and egg mix to remaining egg mixture and mix well. Fold in whipped cream.

Using individual dishes or one large bowl, cover the bottom with Berry Compote (see below), allow to cool.

Add Chocolate Mousse and decorate.

Berry Compote

Use either raspberries or blackberries, can be fresh or frozen.

1 cup of port
½ cup of sugar
¼ cup of kirsch
2 cups of berries
juice of ½ a lemon
½ tsp of cornflour

Bring port, sugar and kirsch to the boil, add berries and lemon juice. Thicken with cornflour.

German Waffles

Barbara Hochstein

This waffle recipe has a long tradition with my family. My grandmother made them using a waffle iron on a coal range in Germany. As a child we would eat them with just icing sugar. When my parents immigrated to New Zealand, we started eating the waffles with fresh strawberries and kiwifruit, sprinkled with sugar. The tradition has carried on with my own family; these waffles are always popular with our son, Nicholas and his friends.

120g butter
50g sugar
3 eggs
zest of lemon
(optional)
250g flour
1 tsp baking powder
250ml milk

Melt the butter and beat together with the sugar and eggs until creamy. Add the lemon zest, and then the flour/baking powder and milk alternatively. Spoon mixture into a waffle machine or cook the mixture in an oiled frying pan like pikelets.

Add sliced strawberries and kiwifruit and sprinkle with icing sugar.

Puha Sauce

Mere Marshall

Puha is delicious. It is a bitter vegetable and for that reason it is probably a natural accompaniment to rich or fatty meats—a boil up favourite. It is essentially, a spinach-type vegetable and that is how I have used it here. It has a little more punch than spinach, I like that—I hope you will, too. This is a simple recipe, easily put together for a week-night meal; nutritious as well as delicious, in my view. For special meals it can be 'flashed up' with toasted nuts and/or blue cheese.

2 tbsp olive oil
1 large onion, chopped
3 cloves garlic
250g puha
¾ tsp nutmeg
2 cups vegetable stock or water
½ cup chopped parsley
½ tsp dried thyme
freshly ground black pepper
pinch of salt
½ cup yoghurt or sour cream
or silken tofu mixed with tsp oil

Wash the puha thoroughly, removing all thick stalks and flower buds, if any. Then rub the leaves together vigorously to crush the leaf membrane. This process prevents the puha from being too bitter—not needed if using silverbeet or spinach. Cut up finely and set aside. Crush the garlic and mix to a paste with the salt. Heat the oil in a heavy-bottomed pan and gently fry the onion and garlic paste until soft. Add the chopped puha and sprinkle the nutmeg over it, then stir the puha through onion and garlic until wilted. Add the stock then cover and simmer for about 5 minutes. Take the lid off and simmer a further 5 minutes until the sauce has thickened a little. Remove from the heat and stir in the pepper, parsley and thyme. Lastly add the yoghurt or sour cream or tofu cream. Serve immediately over pasta, corn cakes or gnocchi.

For special meals try this:
¾ cup walnuts
¼ cup pumpkin seeds
salt

Dry-fry the nuts and seeds in a heavy-bottomed pan, moving them constantly so they don't burn. Place a lid on the pan until the seeds stop popping. Crush the nuts and seeds a little and add salt. Sprinkle over pasta and puha sauce. For those who like cheese over their pasta sauce, add half a cup of parmesan cheese.

Pickled Mushrooms

Heather Heather

This is a recipe from my son, Neil. It is easy to make and the mushrooms are delicious.

200ml red wine vinegar
2 whole cloves
6 tbsp cold water
4 whole black peppercorns
½ bay leaf
1½ tsp salt
2 cloves garlic
500g small fresh mushrooms
1 tbsp vegetable oil

Place the vinegar, cloves, water, peppercorns, bay leaf and crushed garlic into a large stainless steel saucepan. Bring to the boil over a high heat. Drop in mushrooms and reduce heat to low. Simmer uncovered for 10 minutes, stirring occasionally. Leave to cool at room temperature.

Remove the garlic from the marinade. Pour the rest of the contents into a 750ml jar. Slowly pour vegetable oil on top. Place the lid on the jar and secure tightly. Refrigerate for at least a week before serving.

Savoury Scone Slice

This is a different take on the Kiwi bacon and egg pie using a scone dough instead of flaky pastry. On the farm, it was always popular with our shearers for morning tea and it seemed to give them enough energy to shear a further couple of hundred lambs!

Pastry:
2 cups flour
2 tsp baking powder
2 tbsp butter
¼ tsp salt
1 tbsp cider vinegar
½ cup plain yoghurt
½ cup milk

Filling:
300g spinach
pinch nutmeg
6 rashers bacon
8 eggs
100ml cream
pepper
parsley
tomato

Sift together the flour and baking powder, add the melted butter, salt, vinegar and yoghurt. Mix together to a smooth consistency but be careful not to overwork. Wrap in plastic and refrigerate for 15 minutes.

Wash and coarsely chop the spinach, place in a hot pan and season with nutmeg. Place the lid on pan and wilt the spinach quickly. Put spinach to one side. Chop the bacon rashers into 1cm squares. Crack the eggs into a bowl, add cream, and lightly stir to break the yolks but do not whisk.

On a floured surface, roll the dough out to 1cm thick. Line a 20 x 30cm baking dish and refrigerate for 10–15 minutes. Trim the excess pastry from the edges. Fill the pastry case with the spinach, top with bacon, then pour the egg mix over the top. Garnish with sliced tomato, chopped parsley and cracked pepper.

Bake at 200°C for 20 minutes.

Pesto Chicken

Serves 8

150g sundried tomatoes
2 cloves garlic
4 tbsp sweet chilli sauce
2 tbsp chopped parsley
50g grated Parmesan cheese
12 tbsp olive oil
150g roasted cashew nuts
8 chicken legs
salt
1 tbsp olive oil

In a blender, place coarsely-chopped sundried tomatoes, garlic, chilli sauce, parsley, parmesan cheese and olive oil, blend well. Add cashew nuts and pulse briefly. Set half of this pesto mix aside. Trim the chicken legs of excess fat. With your finger, push a cavity between the skin and the meat. Using half of the pesto mix, fill the cavity of each chicken leg with pesto. Season the chicken with salt. Brush an oven tray with olive oil, and heat in a pre heated oven, 200˚C, until hot. Place the chicken legs on the hot tray, skin down, and roast for 15 minutes. Turn and roast for a further 15 minutes. Top with the remaining pesto and roast for another 10 minutes, or until the chicken is completely cooked through.

Pork Piccata Milanese

This is an old, classical recipe from Italy. Traditionally pork is used but this dish is also delicious when cooked with chicken or wild turkey breast. It is very quick and easy to make and children and adults alike will enjoy it.

12 pork medallions
salt
white pepper
flour
2 eggs
1 cup grated parmesan cheese
oil for frying

Season the pork with salt and pepper, then coat with flour. Lightly mix together the eggs and parmesan cheese. Dip the floured medallions into the egg/cheese mix and panfry in hot oil.

Serve on a bed of spaghetti with a fresh tomato sauce.

Mrs Ball's Chutney Chicken

Elise De Bruin

Mrs Ball's chutney is South African chutney available from most New Zealand supermarkets.

1 cup flour
salt and pepper to taste
6 chicken breasts or equivalent
of any other cut of chicken
1 cup oil
1 onion
2 capsicum, any colour
½ cup Mrs Ball's chutney
½ cup tomato sauce
2 cups beef stock
  (Oxo cubes are best)

Put flour, salt and pepper in a plastic bag, add the chicken pieces and shake until all the chicken pieces are covered with flour. Brown the chicken pieces in the oil in a deep frying pan. Once chicken is browned, take the breasts out of the pan and keep aside. Add extra oil to the pan, if necessary, and sauté chopped onion and capsicum. Once sautéed, add the chutney, tomato sauce and beef stock. Add chicken. Cover with a lid and cook approximately 20 minutes or until the chicken is cooked. Extra water can be added if the mixture is too thick.

Serve with steaming rice, a nice salad and a dollop of Mrs Ball's chutney on the side.

- Substitute the flour with gluten-free flour available from all supermarkets.
- Substitute Mrs Ball's chutney with any gluten-free chutney or apricot/peach jam.
- Use gluten-free tomato sauce.
- Substitute the Oxo cubes with Massel gluten-free stock.

Note; that the colour of the gluten-free dish is much lighter than that of the non gluten-free option.

ARTFELT DOLLS
$50.00

Lovo – Earth Oven

Fijian Community

New Zealand has a vibrant Fijian community. The Fijian version of an earth oven, or hangi, is known as a lovo. In Fiji, a lovo is still used by many in the community, especially on Sundays. It is put down before people go to church and the food is ready by the time church finishes. Here in Rotorua, a lovo is put down to mark a special occasion and as fundraising venture. To start, dig a shallow pit and fill with stones. Volcanic rock is best to use as it heats up quickly, doesn't explode and is light to handle. Build a good fire up and over the stones, it takes 2–3 hours for the stones to heat up in the fire—this depends on the size of the lovo and the ferocity of the fire. A sure sign that the stones are hot enough is when they turn white. Wrapped food is placed in baskets on top of the hot stones, and the baskets are then covered with either leaves or foil, layers of wet paper and soil. Once the food is covered the cooking takes approximately two hours. In Fiji they would use coconut and banana leaves instead of aluminium foil to wrap the food and cover the lovo. Food wrapped in leaves is healthier than when wrapped in foil as the fat is able to drain out of the leaves. The most important thing to remember when cooking in a lovo is to cover it well so that the heat cannot escape. Food cooked in a Lovo can be any type of meat, taro, sweet potatoes, yams, palusami (coconut milk wrapped in taro leaves), or stuffed pumpkin. When layering the food in the basket, always make sure you put the heavy, fatty meat at the bottom and the chicken on top.

Stuffed Pumpkin

Mr Simione Waqairatu

1 medium pumpkin
3–4 cans coconut cream
1 large tin corned beef
or tuna
1 onion
2 tomatoes
salt

Cut a lid in to the top of the pumpkin by holding the knife at an angle so that you are able to put the lid back on without it falling in. Remove the seeds and any stringy bits. Bring rest of the ingredients slowly to the boil. Fill the hollowed-out pumpkin with this mixture, replace the lid, and slowly cook in the oven at 150–160°C (or in the lovo) for approximately 1½–2 hours, or until soft.

Huzaren Salad

Agnes Bergs

This is a Dutch recipe for cold meat and vegetables that I got it from my Mother. I have been making this salad for over 50 years. It is good to take to a potluck lunch or barbecue.

6 potatoes
200g cooked meat, beef,
chicken or lamb
300g peas
1 carrot
1 onion
2 gherkins
½ tsp salt
mayonnaise
4 boiled eggs
tomatoes
avocado

In a large bowl put finely-chopped cooked potatoes, diced meat, cooked peas, grated carrot and finely chopped onion and gherkins. Season with salt. Add enough mayonnaise to combine and add some gherkin juice.

Arrange some large lettuce leaves on a serving platter, place salad in the middle. Garnish with peeled and halved boiled eggs, tomato wedges and sliced avocado.

You can keep the salad in the fridge, but remove an hour before serving.

Asian Noodle Salad

1 carrot
2 courgettes
50g snow peas
1 red pepper
2 spring onions
½ cup roasted salted peanuts
400g fresh Udon noodles
handful freshly chopped coriander

Marinade:
½ cup orange juice
zest of 1 orange
juice and zest of 1 lime
5 tbsp rice wine vinegar
3 tbsp fish sauce
3 tbsp soya sauce
½ cup sesame oil
1 tbsp palm sugar
2 finely chopped mild chillies
3 tbsp finely grated root ginger

Cut the carrot and courgettes into long, thin batons and slice the snow peas on the diagonal. Blanch quickly, 3-4 minutes in boiling water. Remove and rinse with cold water. Add the Udon noodles to the boiling water and cook for 1-2 minutes. Remove and rinse with cold water. Slice the red pepper into batons, thinly slice spring onions diagonally.

Combine all the ingredients with marinade and serve.

*Food is the beginning of wisdom.
The first condition of putting anything into your head and heart.*

Anonymous

Warm Purple Potato Salad

1 kg purple potatoes
1 red onion
1 cup chicken stock
1 tbsp Dijon mustard
6–8 tbsp sunflower oil
3–4 tbsp cider vinegar
salt
freshly ground pepper
250g smokey pork sausages
1 cup baby rocket leaves

Boil the potatoes in their jackets in salted water. Once cooked and while still hot, peel and cut into 3cm cubes. Put warm potatoes in a large bowl, season with salt and pepper and add thinly sliced onion, mustard, hot chicken stock, vinegar and oil.

Slice sausages into 3–4mm slices and quickly brown in a hot pan.

Arrange the warm potato salad on a serving plate, top with baby rocket leaves and sliced sausage.

You can also use sliced black pudding instead of the sausage.

Serve warm or cold.

Beef Stroganoff

Serves 4-6

600g beef schnitzel
salt
pepper
1 tbsp Worcester sauce
1 tbsp Dijon mustard
1 onion
2 tbsp oil
2 tbsp butter
200g button mushrooms
1 tbsp tomato paste
1½ cups chicken stock
250g sour cream
3 medium gherkins
1 tbsp sweet paprika

The meat in this dish is cooked quickly like you would for a stir-fry. Slice the schnitzels into 1cm wide strips, season with salt, pepper, Worcester sauce and mustard. Heat oil in a heavy-based pan and quickly cook the beef over a high heat until medium-rare. Remove the meat with a slatted spoon and set aside, keep warm. Reduce the heat to medium, add butter and finely diced onions, sauté for 2–3 minutes, add sliced mushrooms and sauté a further 2–3 minutes. Add tomato paste and then the paprika and sauté 1–2 minutes. Add chicken stock and simmer to reduce the sauce by a third. Add 200g of the sour cream and bring to the boil. Remove the pan from the heat. Add the meat to the sauce and serve garnished with gherkin julienne and the remaining sour cream.

Lebanese Lamb Kafta's

Makes 8-10 kebabs

olive oil
1 onion
3 cloves garlic
4 sundried tomatoes
1 tsp ground cumin
1 tsp ground coriander
¼ tsp ground cinnamon
1 tsp finely chopped mint
1 tbsp milk powder
salt
pepper
500 grams lamb mince
wooden skewers

Soak the skewers in cold water. Sauté the finely chopped onion and garlic in a dash of olive oil until golden and set aside to cool.
In a large bowl, stir together the cooled onion mix with the finely diced sundried tomatoes. Add the rest of the ingredients (keeping the meat cold at all times). Form the mixture around the end of the skewers and grill in a griddle pan or on the barbecue, turning until lightly charred, approximately 5-6 minutes—be careful not to overcook.

Serve with a crisp green salad and minted yoghurt on the side, or in pita pocket.

Pork Bone Boil-up

June Northcroft Grant

Te Arawa, Mai I Maketu ki Tongariro, Tuhourangi/Ngati Wahiao, Ngati Tuwharetoa

This would undoubtedly be one of the most popular meals in a Maori household in Aotearoa. This is a meal that will feed a family, or a large crowd of *manuhiri* (visitors) arriving at a marae for a particular occasion. There would be very few families who have never savoured the smell, taste and enjoyment of a Pork Bone Boil-up. In the days when farmers did their own home killing, the backbone of the pig would have been boned with plenty of meat around the bones, to put into the pot for a boil-up. Traditionally, the bones would be slow-cooked for a couple of hours to tenderise, with a bit of added salt, and in the last half-hour, vegetables and accompanying delicious puha or watercress, freshly picked, would be added to the pot. Seasonal vegetables would be added, potato's (purple rua's, for great colour and firm consistency), kumara, pumpkin and kamo kamo when in season. During winter months when kamo kamo is unavailable, I use courgettes instead, which is from the same family and tastes as sweet. I also put in spinach with the watercress, as this also sweetens the flavour of the vegetables. For a family boil-up, these are the ingredients:

3 kg meaty pork bones
6 potatoes cut in two
3 kumara cut in two
pumpkin cut for as many
people as eating
4 kamo kamo or
4 courgettes
2 bundles of watercress or
2 bundles of puha, or
a cabbage which is also delicious
6 spinach bunches

Cover the meat with cold water in a large pot. Add salt and slow-boil for 2 hours. Thoroughly wash watercress in fresh water. If using puha, wash thoroughly and twist to bruise the stalks. Add greens to the pot. On top, add potatoes, kumara, pumpkin, and kamo kamo, or courgettes. Increase the heat until the pot is slowly boiling again, then turn heat to simmer and cook further half to three quarters of an hour.

The meal is now ready to serve.

Note: Best cooked the day before, remove excess fat from the top before reheating.

Chicken and Broccoli Oven Dish

Agnes Bergs

500g chicken fillets
or boneless thighs
salt
black pepper
500g broccoli
500g mushrooms
3 cups milk
1½ tbsp flour
grated cheese

Season the chicken with salt and pepper and fry in a frying pan. Remove from the pan and place in an ovenproof dish.

Blanch the broccoli and place this on top of the chicken. Using the milk and flour, make a white sauce in the microwave, and add the mushrooms and grated cheese (use as much or as little as you like). Pour the sauce over the broccoli and top with extra grated cheese.

Place in the oven at 190°C for 30 minutes. Serve with rice.

Thai Chicken Laksa

Lin Schaeffers

Serves 4

2 onions, diced
1 carrot, sliced into batons
2 sticks celery, sliced
3 gloves garlic, chopped
½ knob ginger, grated
2 stalks lemongrass, crushed
½ cup chopped coriander,
leaf and stalks
4 chicken thighs
500ml chicken stock
1 ltr coconut cream
1 tbsp green curry paste
fish sauce
salt and pepper
rice noodles

In a deep saucepan, sweat the onion, carrot, celery, garlic, ginger, coriander and lemongrass in a little oil. Skin and slice the chicken thighs and add to the saucepan, stir over the heat until the chicken has browned. Add the curry paste and cook for approximately 3 minutes to cook out the flavour in the paste. Pour in the chicken stock, coconut cream and a dash of fish sauce. Bring to the boil, turn down the heat and simmer for approximately 10 minutes.

Place the noodles, and if you wish, extra vegetables into serving bowls. Ladle the soup over the top.

Summer

Beverley's Never Fail Pavlova

Beverly Harris

This recipe was given to me as a newlywed in 1971 after a dinner party disaster. I wasted six egg whites and produced something resembling a slab of foam rubber. I have passed this on to everyone who has ever told me they could not make a pavlova and each one has been amazed at their success.

2 egg whites
1 tsp vanilla
1 heaped cup sugar
1 tsp vinegar
4 tbsp boiling water

Place all ingredients into a cake mixer and beat until really, really thick and shiny. While the mixture is beating, place a sheet of lightly greased tin foil (shiny side up) on a cold oven tray. Make a round outline about the size of a side plate, can be slightly bigger as the mixture does expand. Pour the mixture out onto the foil making a nice round even shape. Preheat oven to 190°C, place the tray on the shelf second from the bottom of the oven. Leave for two minutes and then turn the heat off. Leave for one hour before removing.

This produces a lovely crispy outer shell with soft marshmallow centre.

Yummalicous Pancakes

Luisa Egger

I got this recipe when I was 4 years old and my mum showed me how to make them. I always make them on the weekend especially when I have friends staying for a sleepover. I like to eat them with a hazelnut spread and also like them with lemon and sugar. Dad likes to eat them with apricot jam and some of my friends like to have them with maple syrup.

2 cups of flour
3 eggs
pinch of salt
¾ ltr of milk (approximately)
butter

In a large bowl you first put in the flour and then the eggs and salt, lastly add the milk. Mix all the ingredients together until the mixture has no lumps and is quite runny. Put a little butter into a hot pan and ladle the mixture into the pan, one ladle at a time will do. Once it is a light golden colour, flip to cook the other side. Best eaten hot, straight from the pan, with your favourite topping. They are yummy!

Pavlina

Lorraine Hutt

Decadent. I looked the word decadent up in the dictionary and one, and only one, of its meanings is 'self indulgement'—the others are not very nice indeed!

4 egg whites
¾ cup castor sugar
coconut
passionfruit pulp
cream

Beat the four egg whites until stiff, add the sugar and beat again. Sprinkle a baking sheet with castor sugar, spread out the meringue to approximately half an inch thick and sprinkle with coconut. Bake for 8–10 minutes at 175°C. When cold, flip onto a tea towel and fill with whipped cream. I put passionfruit on top of the cream, but any fruit will do, even tinned fruit. Roll up like a swiss roll—care needs to be taken with this step.

Irish Cream Liqueur

Albert Vallant

3 eggs
300ml cream
1 tin condensed milk
100ml whiskey (or more!)
1 tsp coffee
1 tsp Milo
vanilla essence

Mix everything together, tastes best after a few days. Drink as is, or poured over vanilla ice cream.

Passion Fruit Cream

Tricia Vickers
#

1 cup sugar
1 cup water
1 tbsp gelatine
8–10 passionfruit pulp
½ cup cream

Heat water, sugar and gelatine till dissolved. Cool until nearly set, then beat until thick. Add the passionfruit pulp. Whip the cream and fold in.

Turn into individual dishes or one large glass bowl.

Serve with fruit and/or ice cream. Delectable!

Joy Barrowman
has been making
Christmas Cake's
to be raffled by
Friends of Hospice
for the last 14 years.

Joy's Honey Fruit Cake

Joy Barrowman

Joy has been making this Christmas Cake, to be raffled by Friends of Hospice Rotorua, for the last 14 years. She acquired the recipe over 40 years ago when she was invited to lead a cake decorating course in New Plymouth. The recipe comes from a farmer's wife who was on the course. It keeps for ages (if you can keep those fingers out of the tin!).

1250g mixed fruit
sherry
1 cup honey
250g butter
2 tbsp golden syrup
500g flour
1 cup boiling milk
1 tsp baking soda

Soak the fruit in a glass of sherry the night before. Dissolve next three ingredients together and add to the fruit. Add the flour and then the baking soda dissolved in milk. Put into a 23cm lined tin. Use the spatula and water to smooth the top and to get it nice and shiny. Preheat the oven to 200°C, and turn back to 130°C when the cake is in the oven. Bake for 3 hours. Allow to cool in oven overnight.

If you choose not to soak the fruit in sherry, an alternative is to add 2 teaspoons of essence to the mix, this can be vanilla, rum or almond essence.

Chocolate Chip Almond Cookies

Makes approximately 40 medium sized cookies.

250g butter
½ cup caster sugar
6 tbsp yogurt
2 cups of flour
1 cup finely ground almonds
2 tbsp baking powder
1 cup chocolate chips
vanilla essence
dash of rum

Cream together softened butter and sugar, add yogurt, vanilla and rum. Sift flour and baking powder together, add almonds and chocolate chips and mix. Add the dry ingredients to the creamed butter and fold together.

Shape as desired and bake at 180°C for approximately 20 minutes.

Gifts of time and love are surely the basic ingredients of a truly merry Christmas.

Peg Bracken

Christmas Cheer Cake

Betty Whitehouse

1 cup butter
1 cup sugar
4 eggs
1 cup dried fruit
lemon juice
nuts
1 tsp baking powder
1 tsp baking soda
1 tsp salt
1 cup brown sugar
1-2 quarts whisky

Before you start, sample the whiskey to check for quality. Good isn't it? Now go ahead, select a large mixing bowl, measuring cup etc., Check the whiskey again as it must be just right. To be sure it is of the highest quality, pour a level cup into a glass and drink this as fast as you can. Repeat. With an electric mixer beat one cup of butter in the large fluffy bowl, add a tsp of thugar and beat again. Meanwhile make sure the whiskey is of the finest quality. Cry another tup. Open second quart if necessary. Add 2 arge legs, 2 tups of fried druit and beat til high.If druit gets stuck in the beaters, just pry it loose with a drewdriver. Sample whiskey again, checking for tonscisticity. Next fift 3 cups of salt or anything else, it really doesn't matter. Sample the whiskey. Ftft one pint of lemon juice. Fold in chopped butter and strained nuts. Add a babblespon of brown sugar, or whatever colour you like, mix well. Grease the oven and turn cake pan to 350 degrees. Now pour the whole mess into the oven and fake. *Check the whiskey again and bo togged.*

Best of luck and hope you sober up in time for Christmas.

This recipe was published in the 1992 Friends of Hospice recipe book, Friends Favourite Food.

Fruit Balls

Rosie Waller

1½ tbsp margarine or butter
½ teaspoon vanilla
125g dates
2 eggs
1½ cup crushed cornflakes
1 apple
½ cup coconut

Melt the butter in a pot and add finely chopped dates. Cook over a low heat until soft. Add beaten eggs, grated apple, cornflakes, coconut, and vanilla. Place in the refrigerator to chill.

Roll into 44 balls and either put back covered in the fridge until firm. or bake at 180°C for 15 minutes, eat chilled.

Apricot Balls

Wendy Lewis

This is a very simple favourite Christmas recipe. It was given to me by my then neighbour some 25 years ago and I make at least 3 batches every year. They were always great to take somewhere when the kids were younger. I still make them; in fact the recipe is still on its original piece of paper!

500g apricots (dried)
1 cup coconut
1 tin condensed milk
grated lemon rind

Mince apricots, add remaining ingredients, and roll into balls in extra coconut. Chill.

Date and Almond Balls

Britta Noske

1½ cups whole almonds, skins on
2 cups pitted fresh dates
1 tsp pure vanilla essence
raw cocoa powder

Place in food processor, ½ cup of almonds and process to a fine meal. Set aside. Roughly chop dates, place with the remaining almonds and vanilla in the processor, and process until well combined. Using a heaped teaspoon of the mixture, mould the paste into a ball, and roll in the reserved almond meal, or cocoa, (or both).

Balls should be kept small as this mixture is very rich.

Balls can be stored for up to 4 days in the refrigerator and are ideal for school lunches or snacks.

Hautapu Fruit Cake

Maree Tombleson

I was given this recipe by Betty Morgan, many years ago. Betty and her husband had a farm at Hihitahi, north of Taihape and my husband Ted worked on it after the war. Also known as the 'listening cake', as you put the cake to your ear to see if it is cooked—if you hear bubbling it is not ready. This is a simple and delicious afternoon tea cake.

½ lb butter
½ lb sugar
2 eggs
1 pkt mixed fruit
1 small teacup milk
¾ lb flour
1 tsp baking powder
1 tsp golden syrup

Cream together the butter and sugar, slowly add the eggs mixing well. Dissolve the golden syrup in the milk. In a separate bowl sift the flour and baking powder, and then crumble in the dried fruit. Fold the flour/fruit mixture into the creamed sugar and butter, alternating with the milk.

Bake about 1–1½ hours (no more than 2) at 325˚F (166˚C).

Spontaneous Mango Ice Cream

Judy Oberhumer

This recipe is a favourite in our household, the lemon/sugar ratio can be adjusted depending on how sweet the mangos are. Depending on the time of year some are super sweet so I would only use ¼ cup sugar and the mango and lemon juice for the liquid. I'm not very good at exact measurements but ice cream makers are very forgiving.

400ml mango puree
⅓ cup icing sugar
2 lemons
300ml cream
500–600ml liquid nitrogen
  (optional)

In a food processor, puree the fresh mangoes (you can also use tinned ones although fresh ones are best), then strain through a fine sieve. Add the sugar and finely grated lemon rind and juice. In a separate bowl, whisk the cream until just starting to thicken. Fold the cream into the mango mix and taste. Add more sugar if required, this will depend on the sweetness of the mangoes. Put into an ice cream maker or have some fun with and make it with liquid nitrogen.

With liquid nitrogen: put the mango mixture into a stainless steel bowl, put on your safety goggles and go outside. Add one third of the liquid nitrogen to the mango mixture and stir vigorously with a wooden spoon. Once smooth add another third of liquid nitrogen and keep on stirring vigorously. Now is the time to have the first taste, it might be ready and frozen enough—if not quite there yet, carry on with the last third of nitrogen until you have the right consistency.

Best served with fresh berries.

Melon Granita

Granita is an easy, delicious and refreshing frozen dessert ideal for summer. This recipe uses honey dew melon but you could use other fruits.

600g honey dew melon
200ml water
100g caster sugar
300ml sparkling white wine

Peel and de-seed the melon and put into a food processor with the sugar and water. Pulse until smooth. Add the wine and freeze with liquid nitrogen as described in the Mango Ice Cream recipe above. If liquid nitrogen is not available, pour into a container approximately 2cm thick and freeze. Stir occasionally with a fork to break the forming crystals. Once frozen into crystals you can store in the freezer until ready to serve.

Serve as a palette cleanser between courses or with fruit as a dessert.

French Strawberry Ice Cream

Tessa Duder

Serves 6

On a recent trip to Rotorua, I was delighted to discover in the Government Gardens a newly-erected bust of my French ancestor Camille Malfroy. I'd always known that my father's great-uncle had been a prominent figure in the city's early development, but not in any great detail. In Rotorua the name continues for roads, schools, a motel, bakery and other businesses.

1 cup caster sugar
pinch salt
3 egg yolks
1 cup standard milk
2 heaped cups sliced strawberries
(smaller are often sweeter)
1 cup cream
1 tsp vanilla essence

Make custard: Put half a cup of caster sugar, salt and egg yolks into a medium sized bowl and whisk until smooth. Heat the milk until almost boiling and gradually add to the egg-yolk mixture. Put bowl over (not in) saucepan of boiling water and stir constantly until mixture is lightly thickened. Set custard aside until cold.

Put strawberries and half a cup of caster sugar into a processor and pulse. Strain this puree through a sieve, (slightly tedious but necessary to get rid of the pips for the desired creamy texture). Combine the cooled custard with the puree, pour into a wide shallow covered container and put in the freezer.

When the mixture is partly frozen, put into a medium-sized bowl and stir with a fork. Whip the cream and vanilla until soft and floppy. Fold the cream into the ice cream, return to the container and freeze until softly frozen. Scoop into a chilled processor bowl and pulse until smooth but not melted. (You can use an electric beater for this). Return to the container and freeze for at least 24 hours.

"there's nothing nicer to eat under a
sun umbrella than home-made ice cream."

Beans, Bacon and Orange

Averil Ann Bateman

I first cooked this recipe in 1964, the year Andrew was born. We were living at Riverside Close, Staines, Middlesex.

1 onion
1 large capsicum
olive oil
4 rashers bacon
2 large mushrooms
1 can baked beans
1 orange

Slice the onion and soften in the microwave for one minute, set aside. Treat the capsicum the same way. Splash the olive oil in a large frying pan, dice the bacon and fry lightly. Add the peeled and sliced mushrooms and fry for half a minute. Add the onion and capsicum, and then add the can of baked beans and peeled and diced orange. Cook for a minute or until heated through. Do not overcook.

Serve alone or with crusty bread and a green salad.

Tofu Burgers

Rosie Waller

250g tofu
1 medium onion
2 cloves garlic
¼ tsp ground ginger
¼ sunflower seeds
1 tbsp dark soy sauce
1 tbsp nutritional yeast
¼ cup wholemeal flour
oil for frying

Drain any moisture off the tofu. Dice the onion and garlic very finely. Crumble the tofu into a bowl, add onion and garlic, then add the remaining ingredients. Add a little water and lemon juice if too thick. Mix well. Wet your hands and then divide the mixture into 8 x 7–10cm patties.

Heat oil in a frying pan and cook the patties for 5 minutes each side or until golden.

Cheese Puffs

Anne Reynolds

Quick and easy to make, best eaten on the day.

3 cups sifted flour
4 tsp baking powder
3 cups grated cheese
2 eggs
¾ cup milk

Combine the flour, baking powder and cheese. Beat the eggs and combine with milk. Blend with the dry ingredients (you may need to use a little extra milk).

Place spoonfuls of the mixture onto a well greased tray and bake in a preheated oven at 220˚C for approximately 10 minutes.

Zucchini Slice

Ynes Fraser

This is an excellent, simple recipe which I often use for a luncheon with a salad and it always seems to be acceptable. I hope you will find it so. Can be made a day ahead and stored overnight in the fridge, reheat to serve.

400g zucchini
1 level cup flour
2 tsp baking powder
½ cup grated cheese
salt
pepper
1 onion
2 rashers bacon
1 tbsp butter
3 large eggs
½ cup oil
red capsicum (optional)
parmesan cheese
paprika

Combine in a bowl grated zucchini, flour, baking powder, cheese, salt and pepper. Sauté in butter, finely sliced onion and bacon. Beat together the eggs and oil. Add the eggs to zucchini, onion/bacon mixture, and then add finely diced red capsicum. Combine.

Pour into a greased 23cm dish. Sprinkle with parmesan cheese and paprika. Bake at 180°C for about 35 minutes.

Courgette Fritters

Serves 4

2 eggs
1 clove garlic
½ tsp salt
3 cups grated courgette
¼ cup of grated tasty cheese
½ cup flour
½ tsp baking powder

Beat the eggs until light and frothy. Crush the garlic clove and the salt together until it turns to a paste and add to the egg mixture. Combine grated courgette and tasty cheese together with the egg. Add flour and baking powder, folding until you have a light batter. Preheat oil in a frying pan, spoon in mixture and cook, turning when golden brown.

Serve on a plate with Tangy Tomato Sauce (see recipe below).

Tangy Tomato Sauce

1 medium onion, finely chopped
2 cloves garlic
2 tsp brown sugar
1 can chopped tomatoes
¼ cup of sweet chilli sauce
finely grated lemon zest

Sauté in a pan, the chopped onion and garlic over a medium heat until translucent. Add sugar and allow to caramelise.
Add tomatoes and chilli sauce, cook slowly over a low heat until thick.

Before serving add finely grated lemon zest.

Warm Polenta & Grilled Vegetables

Polenta is extremely versatile, serve it creamy with winter stews instead of rice or potatoes or as in this recipe, grilled with a variety of summer vegetables. You can use any combination that you like, vary the combinations depending on what is available in the garden. Serve warm, or if you prefer cold, drizzle with a light balsamic and olive oil dressing.

6 cups of water
salt
2 cups polenta
3 tbsp butter
olive oil
1 aubergine
3 coloured capsicums
3 courgettes,
4 chilli's (optional)
ground black pepper
salt
shaved parmesan

Bring water and salt to boil and slowly add the polenta, stirring constantly. Cover and allow to simmer for 10 minutes stirring occasionally. Add the butter. Pour the Polenta onto a greased tray and spread evenly, approximately 2cm thick. Once cool, cut into wedges.

Preheat the oven grill or barbecue. Remove the seeds from the capsicums and slice all the vegetables into thick slices. Place the vegetables and polenta wedges on a lightly greased oven tray, sprinkle with rock salt and brush lightly with olive oil. Grill or barbecue until well coloured.

Arrange on a platter, the wedges of polenta, topped with grilled vegetables and shaved parmesan.

Ricotta and Pesto Torte

Joanne Bryant

This is a favourite of mine, adapted from a recipe of Ruth Petty's, it is always popular when served with drinks before the meal.

350g cream cheese
200g ricotta cheese
175g unsalted butter
¼ cup sun-dried tomatoes
½ cup lightly toasted walnuts
100g basil pesto

Allow cream cheese and ricotta to come to room temperature. Process cream cheese until smooth. Add melted butter and process until combined. Add ricotta and briefly pulse to combine. Divide mixture into two as the torte will have 2 layers.

Line a bowl, approximately 5–6 inch in diameter with plastic wrap. Place a circle of sundried tomatoes, in the base of the bowl. Spread first layer of cheese mix and smooth. Cover this first layer with basil pesto and smooth off. Spread second layer of cheese mix and cover this with coarsely chopped walnuts, keep 4–5 halves for garnish. Chill for at least one hour before serving.

Serve with crostini, toasted pita bread or crudities.

"Then followed that beautiful season.......summer"
Anonymous

Basil Pesto

1 clove garlic
50g pine nuts
45g basil leaves
45g grated parmesan
¼ cup olive oil
salt
white pepper
lemon juice to taste

Place garlic, pine nuts, basil and parmesan into a food processor and process until smooth. Slowly pour in olive oil with the processor on low pulse.

Add salt, pepper and lemon juice to taste.

Beef Stir-fry with Black Bean Sauce

Sarah Walker
BMX World Champion

500g lean beef schnitzel
2 tbsp dark soy sauce
1 onion
2 stalks celery
3 tsp garlic
150g mushrooms
100g snow peas
  or green beans
1–2 tbsp black bean
and garlic sauce

Cut the beef across the grain into thin strips. Mix with 1 tablespoon of dark soy sauce and a seasoning of pepper. Cover and set aside for 5–10 minutes. Heat a dash of oil in a large wok or frying pan. Over a high heat stir-fry the beef in two or three batches, until just browned. Remove meat as it browns. Do not overcook. Reduce the heat, stir-fry the sliced onion for a few minutes then add the thinly sliced celery, minced garlic, sliced mushrooms, snow peas and beef with the remaining soy sauce and black bean and garlic sauce. Stir or toss well until very hot.

Serve immediately with rice or noodles.

Corn Cakes, Avocado Whip and Bacon

Rosie Waller

500g corn kernels
3 tbsp olive oil
sea salt
fresh milled pepper
75ml milk, heated
50g flour
¼ cup flat-leaf parsley
½ tbsp crushed chilli
½ lemon, zested
4 egg whites
avocado, chopped
1 lemon, juiced
3 tbsp sour cream, whipped
6 bacon rashers,

Shave the corn kernels off the cob, coat the corn in olive oil, season and warm through. Divide corn into two thirds and one third. In a liquidiser, place in two thirds of the corn, the milk, flour, chilli, parsley and lemon zest. Blitz for 2 minutes. Pour into a mixing bowl. Meanwhile, whip the egg whites to firm peaks then fold through the batter and the remaining corn.

Heat the solid top on the barbecue, spray some egg poaching rings with oil, spoon in the mixture, when sealed, remove rings and turn with a fish slice.

To make the avocado whip; in a food processor, puree the avocado, lemon juice and sour cream until smooth and light.

Cook the bacon until crisp.

Serve the corn cakes with a dollop of avocado whip and top with a rasher of bacon.

Slow Roasted Tomato and Pepper with Horopito

Mere Marshall

This recipe calls for sun-ripened tomatoes. They don't need to be big or cherry varieties although that would be fine too. It is a simple recipe—in fact it is a bit of a cheek calling it a recipe. I have served this dish for breakfast and for dinner, usually accompanied with homemade corn bread or semolina gnocchi or Skirlie and some steamed courgettes.

2 medium tomatoes per person
1 red capsicum per person
olive oil
avocado and horopito oil
lovage or fresh lemon thyme
salt

You may also use 6–8 cherry tomatoes or one large tomato per person, if you can, have them with the green stem attached as it looks attractive. Blister the capsicums and rest them in a bag. Cut the tomatoes in half and place in a roasting dish with the cut side up, drizzle with olive oil and cook in a slow oven for about 40 minutes. The juice from the tomatoes will be sticky. Peel the skin from the capsicums and discard the seeds. Cut into evenly sized pieces.

Arrange on individual plate the sliced capsicum and tomatoes. Sprinkle with chopped lovage or lemon thyme, season with salt. Drizzle with a little of the avocado and horopito oil—remember this is very hot.

Butterflied Leg of Lamb

Mary Mathis

Several years ago my friend, Jenny Corry, and I went to some cooking classes in Auckland. I can't remember the lady's name but it was at a place in Remuera. This is one of the recipes we learnt and since then we have both used this recipe often.

1 butterflied leg of lamb
¼ cup malt vinegar
¼ cup dark soy sauce
2–3 cloves garlic, crushed
2 tbsp brown sugar
½ tsp chilli powder
2 tbsp olive oil
freshly ground pepper
salt

Combine all the ingredients in a plastic bag, add the prepared leg of lamb and marinate for 48 hours, turning every 12 hours. Barbecue each side over a low-medium heat with the lid closed for 15–20 minutes each side. Rest for 5 minutes before slicing, serve with salsa (see recipe below).

Salsa

2 cups soft dates
1 red pepper
½ tsp sambal olek
1 cup chopped parsley
2 sprigs mint
1 lemon
1 tsp root ginger
olive oil
1 banana

The day before: mix together finely chopped dates and red pepper, add sambal olek, parsley and chopped mint. Add rind and juice of lemon, freshly grated ginger and enough olive oil to combine.

Store in refrigerator overnight. Two hours before serving add sliced banana.

Aunty Bea's Curried Chicken

Beatrice Yates (aka Aunty Bea)

Aunty Bea is a well known Rotorua personality, respected teacher and community fundraiser. Aunty Bea is of Te Arawa descent, who is also proud of her Scottish, Irish and Fijian Indian ancestry.

1 onion
8 cloves garlic
1 tbsp olive oil
fresh ginger
3 kg chicken
2 tbsp curry powder
rock salt
1 tsp paprika
1 tsp turmeric
1 tsp garam masala
1 can whole tomatoes
½ cup water
6 large potatoes
2 sprigs mint

Heat the oil in a frying pan and cook the sliced onion, crushed garlic and fresh pounded ginger until lightly brown. Add the chicken (can be chicken wings or boneless chicken cut into pieces) and fry gently for ten minutes. Add the curry powder, salt to taste, paprika, turmeric, garam masala, tomatoes and water. Keep stirring to prevent sticking. Add the potatoes, peeled and cut into quarters, and two sprigs of mint. Cook until chicken is tender and potatoes are cooked.

Serve with rice.

Yoghurt Chicken

Serves 6-8

8 chicken thighs
salt
white pepper
flour
400ml natural yoghurt
1 tsp sweet paprika
1 tsp mild curry
1 tsp coriander
½ tsp cumin
1 lemon, zest and juice
2 cloves garlic, crushed
oil

Trim excess fat from the chicken and season with salt and white pepper, then coat with flour. In a container mix together all other ingredients, add chicken thighs and coat well. Cover and leave in refrigerator for 1–2 hours. Bake in a greased baking dish in the oven at 200˚C for 20–30 minutes or until cooked through.

To serve garnish with lemon zest and freshly chopped coriander.

Beer Butt Chicken

We first heard of cooking chicken this way 6 years ago when visiting friends in Canada, since then we have seen it cooked on barbecue's around New Zealand. A Dutch friend recently lent us a cook book from Holland and they also had it there, a truly international recipe! The beer keeps the chicken moist and gives an added flavour.

1 large chicken
2 rashers bacon
can of beer
salt
pepper

Clean the chicken and dry with a paper towel. Season both the inside and outside of the chicken with salt and pepper. Open a can of beer and have a small sip to make sure it is ok. If you are not sure, finish that one and open a second can. Have a sip, then put the open can of beer onto a hot barbecue plate, slide the chicken onto the open can and place the bacon rashers on top. Go and have another beer with your friends, maybe two or three as the chicken will be ready in 60–70 minutes.

Barbecued Pork Fingers

Carla Porter

Pork fingers are pork ribs but you can also use lamb flaps cut into strips. Great to take to a barbecue as you can prepare the meat beforehand and take it in the marinade to pop on the grill when required.

750g pork fingers
1 pkt Brown Onion Sauce
1 glove garlic, crushed
¼ cup water
1 tbsp root ginger, chopped
2 tsp Worcester sauce
2 tbsp honey
3 tbsp tomato sauce
2 tbsp vinegar
pinch chilli powder

In a large saucepan, cover trimmed pork fingers with water. Bring to the boil and simmer for 20 minutes. Drain, and place in a shallow ovenware dish. Whisk the rest of the ingredients together in a saucepan and bring to the boil, stirring constantly. Pour the sauce over the pork fingers, marinate 1–2 hours turning occasionally.

Bake at 190˚C, basting frequently, for 1 hour or until pork is tender or, pop on the barbecue.

Raw Fish

Turia Jones

You can use any white fish that will hold its shape for this marinated fish dish i.e., snapper, tarakihi.

2–4 kg fish
6–8 lemons
salt
spring onions
red pepper or
tomatoes
1 tin coconut milk

Cut the fish into cubes. Season the fish with salt and cover with lemon juice. Leave to marinate overnight or for at least 2 hours. Drain the marinade off the fish, add the finely chopped spring onions, diced red peppers or diced tomatoes; if using tomatoes scoop the seeds out and dice the flesh only. Lastly add the coconut milk and gently fold to mix.

Note; replace a couple of the lemons with limes adds a lovely flavour. If you wish, leave a little of the marinade in with the fish and mix through the coconut.

Rack of Lamb in Puff Pastry

1 large rack of lamb, trimmed
salt
pepper
oil
1 tbsp butter
200g onions
2 cloves garlic
500g mushrooms
100g pitted black olives
1 lemon
1 tsp chopped rosemary
1 roll of puff pastry
1 egg yolk
egg wash

Season the lamb with salt and pepper, quickly sear the outside in a hot pan, allow to cool. Sauté the finely chopped onions and garlic in butter until soft and golden. Add the coarsely chopped mushrooms, sauté until all liquid has evaporated. Add the coarsely chopped olives, grated rind of lemon, lemon juice and rosemary. Season with salt and pepper, cool slightly, then add egg yolk stirring constantly. Cool. Coat the lamb with the mushroom mix and then wrap in puff pastry. Brush with egg wash.

Preheat the oven to 240°C, place the rack of lamb into the oven and reduce temperature to 180°C, bake for 20–30 minutes. Remove from oven and allow to rest for 5 minutes before slicing.

Ham and Mushroom Fettuccine

Floss and John Walters

About 30 years ago, there was a restaurant here in Rotorua which although operated by a Greek, turned out quite exceptional Italian food. Quite a rollicking sort of place. The more wine that was consumed, the more raucous the singing and perhaps the more forgiving about the food one became. Of all the dishes he presented was one called Ham and Mushroom Fettuccine. Floss and I started Robert Harris in Rotorua, later we moved and created Peppers Cafe at Whakarewarewa where we took some of our food ideas with us. One was this fettuccine dish. Cheap to make, and also very, very quick.

500g fettuccine noodles
600ml fresh cream
2 dessert spoons tomato paste
3 cloves garlic
300g shaved ham
300g button mushrooms

Use either dried fettuccine noodles, of you prefer, the fresh variety. Cook the pasta, drain and set aside. The sauce; you can use either fresh cream, or if the waistline won't handle it, the same amount of evaporated milk. Warm this, and add tomato paste, crushed garlic, sliced or shaved ham and sliced button mushrooms. These quantities can be adjusted according to the amount of sauce you are making.

Now, your imagination can run wild! If you have the desire, rummage through the pantry and add sliced stoned black olives, or perhaps some feta finely sliced, maybe some sun-dried tomatoes that have been given the same treatment. Add all this to the tomato based sauce and simmer until the mushrooms are cooked...about 5 minutes. Combine the pasta and the sauce and serve in individual bowls. Dress the finished dish with, say, finely diced parsley—Italian or curly leaf and have a side dish of salad and some crusty bread.

It's easy, can feed a crowd for very little, and is most moreish. Enjoy!

Ricotta and Tomato Cannelloni

200g instant cannelloni tubes
250g ricotta cheese
250g cream cheese
3 medium potatoes
¼ cup of fresh mint
1 red capsicum
salt
white pepper
pinch of nutmeg
2 cups grated cheese
4 tbsp olive oil

Sauce:
1 onion
3 cloves garlic
2 tbsp raw sugar
2 tbsp tomato paste
2 cans chopped tomatoes
salt

Boil the potatoes in their jackets, once cooked, peel and slice finely. While the potatoes are still warm, mix with finely chopped mint and capsicum, add the rest of the ingredients and season to taste. Mix well. Fill the cannelloni tubes with the cheese mix.

To make the sauce; sauté the chopped onion and crushed garlic in oil. Add the tomato paste and then the raw sugar and stir. Add the cans of chopped tomatoes and salt to taste. Cook for 5 minutes.

Put half the sauce in the base of an oven-proof dish—large enough to hold all the cannelloni. Place the filled cannelloni and top with the remaining sauce. Cover with grated cheese, and then aluminium foil. Bake in oven at 200˚C for 20 minutes.

Remove the foil and cook for a further 10–15 minutes, until the cheese has a nice golden colour.

Aubergine filled with Beef and Tomato

2 tbsp oil
1 onion
4 cloves garlic
500g beef mince
2 tbsp tomato paste
1 tbsp raw sugar
¼ cup red wine
1 can chopped tomatoes
2 bay leaves
¼ cup fresh basil
1 cup grated cheese
salt
pepper
2 medium sized aubergines
lemon

Sauté diced onions and chopped garlic until golden. Add the mince and sauté for a further 5 minutes or until all the meat clumps have fallen apart. Add the tomato paste, raw sugar, red wine, full tin of tomatoes and bay leaves. Simmer, stirring occasionally until all the liquid has evaporated. Cut the aubergines in half lengthwise and scoop out the flesh leaving approximately 1cm. Dice the removed aubergine flesh. Rub the aubergine with a little lemon juice. Once the liquid has evaporated from the meat mixture, remove the bay leaves and add the diced aubergine and coarsely chopped basil. Place the aubergine halves in an oven proof dish, sprinkle with salt and fill with the meat mixture. Top with cheese.

Bake in the oven for approximately 20 minutes at 200˚C, or until the aubergines are cooked.

Kumara and Salmon Fritters

Denise La Grouw

This recipe has no real significance except that the mix of kumara, fresh herbs and tinned salmon is delicious! It is best people play with the recipe to get the best flavour for them. My son loves them—they are a good recipe for our home grown kumara and I made it up myself.

1½ cups grated kumara
200g tinned salmon in oil
1 spring onion
handful of fresh chives and parsley (optional)
small chilli (optional)
1 egg
1 tbsp flour
splash of milk as required
salt
pepper
olive oil

Peel and grate the kumara, finely chop the spring onion, chives, parsley and chilli. Place, with the rest of the ingredients in a bowl and mix well, add a splash of milk and season to taste. Heat pan, add oil and place spoonfuls of mixture to cook in a paddy shape. Reduce heat and cook slowly to ensure the kumara is cooked.

Drain oil on paper towels, and serve immediately.

It's about teaching the children to garden and growing vegetables for the people in the village.
Tuhipo Kereopa

Surimi Mornay

Beatrice Yates (aka Aunty Bea)

Serves 4–5

100g butter
1 onion
3 cloves garlic
1 kg surimi crabmeat
1 ltr milk
2 lemons
4-5 slices cheese
salt
pepper
250mls cream
flour to thicken
2 tomatoes
grated cheese

Melt the butter in a frying pan and fry the sliced onion and crushed garlic until a light brown. Add the crab meat and cook slowly for 5 minutes. Add the milk and cook for a further 5 minutes. Squeeze in juice from the lemons and stir. Add the sliced cheese (2 different flavours is best) and cook until the cheese has melted. Pour in the cream, salt and pepper to taste. Sprinkle in the flour and cook, Stirring occasionally, until nicely thickened. Pour into a casserole dish, top with sliced tomatoes and grated cheese. Place in the oven under the grill until nicely browned.

Serve with rice.

Autumn

Autumn Food

Creamy Kumara and Blue Vein Soup

Serves 6-8

10g butter
150g onions
750g kumara
1.25 ltr chicken stock
100g blue vein cheese
200ml cream
salt
white pepper
nutmeg
8-10 saffron strains (optional)
pickle marsala to garnish

Sauté the diced onions in butter, without colouring them. Add the peeled diced kumara and chicken stock, and slowly simmer until the kumara are very soft.

Dice half the blue vein into small cubes for garnish (use a thin bladed knife and hot water), and add the rest to the soup. Process the soup in a food processor until smooth. Return to the heat, add the cream and adjust the seasoning with salt, pepper and nutmeg.

Serve garnished with diced blue vein and a sprinkle of pickle marsala.

Note; Pickle marsala is hot and spicy so use sparingly.

This-and-That Bread

Shona Jennings

The basic recipe for this scone/bread was developed in the Cook Islands by my friend Annie Bonza. I like it because it's one of those recipes you can easily play with— just substitute the coconut for oat bran or rolled oats, and change the spices, fruit and nuts to suit whatever else you're cooking (Annie's recipe uses cardamom, cloves and cinnamon). The Asia-Pacific version, below, tastes great with a generous spread of coriander pesto, served beside a kumara soup or salad.

1 cup shredded coconut
2 cups wholemeal flour
¾ cup white flour
2 tsp baking powder
¾ tsp salt
1 tsp sugar
½ tsp ginger
2 tsp curry powder
1 tsp ground cumin
3 dried apricots, finely chopped
handful sultanas
handful slivered almonds
3 tbsp oil
1 clove garlic
2 tbsp mango chutney
2 cups water

Sift the dry ingredients together in a large bowl. Make a well in the centre, and add the oil. In a separate bowl or jug, stir the crushed garlic and chutney into the water until well dispersed. Add this liquid to the dry mix and oil, and gently stir with a knife until the ingredients are just blended (do not over-mix).

Place mixture into a greased and floured 23cm quiche dish. Brush the top with oil, sprinkle the bread with slivered almonds or sunflower seeds and cut, wagon-wheel style, into eight.

Bake in the oven at 200°C for 30 minutes.

Baked French Onion Soup

Serves 4–6

400g onions
1 clove garlic
30g butter
800ml chicken stock
double shot brandy
50ml white wine
1 bay leaf
salt
nutmeg
thyme leaves
puff pastry
egg yolk
parmesan cheese

Finely slice the onions and sauté with the chopped garlic in butter, until a rich golden colour. Add the brandy, white wine, and then the chicken stock. Add the bay leaf and simmer for 5 minutes. Season to taste with salt and nutmeg, and remove the bay leaf. Fill soup bowls to 2/3 and sprinkle with a pinch of finely chopped thyme leaves and chill.

Cut out circles of puff pastry, 2cm wider than the diameter of the soup bowls. Brush the outside rim of the bowls, approximately ½ cm wide with egg yolk. Place the circle of puff pastry over the top of the bowl and push firmly around the sides of the bowl. Brush the pastry top with egg yolk and sprinkle with finely grated parmesan cheese.

Note; Do not prick the pastry. Bake in the oven at 200°C for approximately 15 minutes depending on the size of the cup.

Lemon Curd Cake

I love making this cake, the basic recipe uses lemon curd. I found it in a Cuisine magazine several years ago and have adapted it. You can change the cake by adding sour cream to the curd to make it creamier and/or put fruit on top of the lemon curd – halved red plums or rhubarb seem to work best. I always make two cakes as that uses up all the lemon curd, and freeze one.

Lemon Curd:
4 large lemons
100g butter
2 cups sugar
4 eggs

Cake:
2 cups self raising flour
1 cup sugar
100g butter
2 tsp rum
2 eggs

Lemon Curd: place the lemon juice, finely grated rind, sugar, and cubed butter into a saucepan. Stir over a low heat until the butter has melted (be careful not to boil). Remove from heat and add beaten eggs. Stir well and return to heat, stirring constantly for 6-8 minutes or until the mixture has thickened. Remove from heat and allow to cool.

Cake: place flour, sugar and cubed butter into a food processor or mixer and blend/mix until the mix resembles fine breadcrumbs. In a separate bowl, lightly beat eggs and add rum. Pour slowly into the flour mix and process to a soft dough.

Grease and line a 23cm tin. Press half the dough into the base. Pour in ½ the curd mixture, and top with remaining crumble.

Note: If you wish to add sour cream, mix together 125g tub of sour cream with cooled lemon curd before pouring into cake tin.

Note: If adding fruit, place fruit on top of lemon curd and then top with remaining dough.

Bake at 180°C for 40-45 minutes or until baked.

Bread and Apple Meringue Pudding

6 thick slices of white bread
½ ltr milk
2 eggs
50g raisins
20g ground almonds
80g melted butter
80g sugar
500g granny smith apples
juice and rind of 1 lemon
1 tsp cinnamon

Meringue:
3 egg whites
75g castor sugar
pinch of salt

Grease an oblong oven proof dish, approximate size 20–30cms. Whisk egg and milk together. Soak half of the bread briefly in the egg mix and place a single layer in the dish. Peel and core the apples and then finely slice them. Combine with the rest of the ingredients and layer on top of the bread. Soak remaining bread in egg mix and layer on top.

Meringue; whisk egg whites and salt till soft peaks form. Slowly add sugar and continue to whisk until stiff.

Smooth meringue on top and bake for 45 minutes at 100˚C.

If necessary, colour meringue under the grill at end—be careful not to let it burn!

Dutch Ginger Cake

Carla Porter

1¾ cups plain flour
¼ tsp salt
125g preserved ginger
1 egg
185g butter
1 cup caster sugar
60g blanched almonds

Sift flour and salt, add sugar and chopped ginger. Melt butter over a gentle heat; allow to cool slightly. Mix in beaten egg, reserving one teaspoon of egg mix for glazing. Add the cooled butter to flour and mix well. Press mixture into a greased tin. Brush top with reserved egg mix and arrange almonds.

Bake at 180˚C for 45 minutes. Allow to cool in the tin before cutting into small wedges.

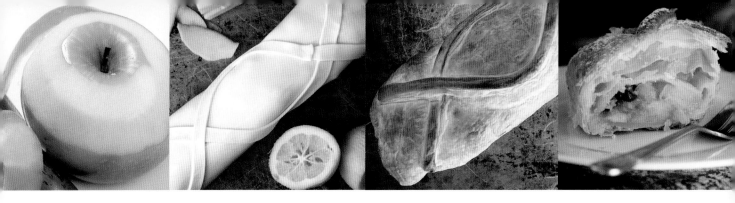

Apfelstrudel

50g white bread crumbs
50g butter
1 kg granny smith apples
70g sugar
30g raisins
juice and rind of 1 lemon
1 tsp vanilla essence
½ tsp ground cinnamon
1 roll of 350 grams puff pastry
egg wash

Sauté breadcrumbs in butter until golden. Peel and core apples and slice thinly. Add all remaining ingredients and mix well. Lay out the roll of puff pastry and spread breadcrumbs over one-third. Lay apple mixture on top of breadcrumbs and roll up tightly.

Place on greased oven tray, glaze with egg wash. Preheat the oven to 220°C, place the strudel in oven and reduce temperature to 180°C, bake for 40 minutes.

Serve warm or cold, with vanilla ice cream or thick cream.

DANGER
THERMAL ACTIVITY
KEEP TO WALKING TRACKS
AT ALL TIMES

Celebration Chocolate Cake

Ruth O'Leary

I make this cake any time there is a birthday or celebration as it never fails and is always impressive! It is slightly adapted from a recipe by Annabel Langbein in her book Cooking to Impress Without Stress. I like to use Valrhona cocoa for this— expensive but so delicious!

2 cups sugar
2 large eggs
1 cup milk
¾ cup of cocoa
200g softened butter
1½ tsp vanilla
¼ tsp salt
3 cups plain flour
3 tsp baking powder
1 cup boiling hot coffee

Place all of the ingredients in a bowl, mix with an electric beater or food processor. Pour the mixture into a greased and lined 30cm tin (I usually use a 23cm tin but it does require a little extra cooking time), and smooth the top. Bake at 160°C for one hour or until a skewer inserted into the centre comes out clean. Cool the cake in the tin, then, when it is cooled, remove and ice the cake with chocolate icing or ganache.

You will never find time for anything.
If you want time, you must make it.
Charles Buxton

Earl Grey Tea Bread

Rosie Waller

Makes 20 large slices

1 cup currants
1½ cups mixed dried fruit
¾ cup cold strong Earl Grey
or Lady Grey tea
1 tbsp treacle or golden syrup
1 egg
¾ cup Equal Spoonful
2 cups self-raising flour
1 tsp mixed spice

Place dried fruit in a large bowl, pour over tea and stir in treacle. Cover and allow to soak overnight. Lightly beat the egg and stir into the fruit mixture, followed by the Equal, the sifted flour and spice.

Spoon into lined 13 x 22cm loaf tin and bake at 160°C for 1–1¼ hours or until a skewer inserted in the centre come out clean.

Cooking on the Marae

The following recipes are from Iri Te Kowhai, Ngati Whakaue, photograph below left. Used on the marae when cooking for hundreds and, at times, thousands, of people. They have been written down from memory. "I don't write recipes down.........I'm a slapper; I slap it altogether."

Iri is very much the boss of the kitchen, and has everything running quietly and orderly. She is used to catering for large crowds, and was in charge of the catering for the 10,000 plus people who attended the tangi's of both Sir Howard Morrison and Taini Morrison. Her largest sit-down banquet was for 550 people. She also catered for 1600 people per day, over three days, at the New Zealand Maori Bowls Tournament. As you will see from the ingredients, Iri is used to cooking in large quantities!

Steam Pudding
Iri Te Kowhai

8 kg butter
24 cups sugar
1 can golden syrup
2 ltr hot milk
6 heaped dessert spoons
baking soda
5 kg flour
1 pkt baking powder
4 x 2 ltr cold milk

Melt butter and add sugar, dissolve baking soda in hot milk. Whisk all ingredients together until smooth.

Line 9 x 3kg large tins with bread bags, fill to three quarters. Tie a knot in the top of the bag, leaving plenty of room for pudding to raise.

Steam for 5 hours.

Caramel Dumplings

Iri Te Kowhai

Iri created this recipe as an alternative to steam pudding to serve on the marae.

Dumplings:
10 cups self-raising flour
3 cups brown sugar
½ ltr warm milk

Mix together until the mixture has a scone texture.

Caramel Sauce:
10 cups hot water
2 cups brown sugar
1 cup golden syrup
500g butter

Bring ingredients to the boil. Pour syrup into a large oblong serving dish. Roll the dumpling mixture into balls and drop into the syrup. Cover with foil and cook in steam-box for 1 hour. Serve with ice cream and whipped cream.

Iri's Pavlova

Iri Te Kowhai

8 egg whites
2 cups caster sugar
1 dessert spoon vanilla essence
1 dessert spoon vinegar

Beat ingredients together at high speed until very stiff. Spread on baking paper and shape into a 25cm disc. Bake at 150°C for ½ hour, then 100°C for 1 hour. Turn oven off and allow the pavlova to cool in the oven.

Kiwi Soda Bread

All these measurements are approximate.

500g flour
1 tsp sugar (optional)
1 tsp salt
1 tsp horopito
1 tsp bicarbonate of soda
200–300ml milk
1 tsp vinegar
8 piko piko

Sift the dry ingredients together in a large bowl, ensuring the bicarbonate of soda is evenly distributed. Make a well in the centre, pour about three-quarters of the milk and vinegar in, and start stirring. You are trying to achieve a dough that is raggy and very soft, but the lumps and rags of it should look dryish and "floury", while still being extremely squishy if you poke them. Add more liquid sparingly if you think you need it.

Turn the contents of the bowl out immediately onto a lightly floured board or work surface, and start to knead.

The main objective here is speed; the chemical reaction of the bicarb with the milk starts as soon as they meet, and you want to get the bread into the oven while the reaction is still running on "high". Don't over-knead! You do not want the traditional "smooth, elastic" ball of dough you would expect with a yeast bread. You should not spend more than half a minute or so kneading, the less time, the better. Don't be concerned if the dough is somewhat sticky; flour your hands, and the dough, and keep going as quickly as you can.

Flatten the dough to a circle of 15–18 centimetres in diameter, place on a floured baking tray, garnish with piko piko. Place the bread into a preheated oven at 200˚C for 45 minutes.

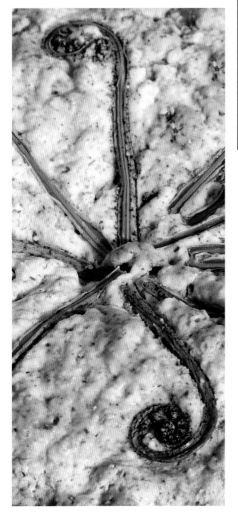

Energiser Bar

2 cups rolled oats
1 cup mixed chopped nuts
(peanuts, almonds, walnuts, cashews)
1 cup shredded coconut
⅓up butter
⅓up brown sugar
¼ cup honey
¼ cup golden syrup
1 cup raisins
1 cup dried banana chips or
  chopped dried apricots

In a roasting dish, combine rolled oats, nuts, and coconut. Toast until nice and golden, stirring occasionally. Be careful not to burn!

In a large saucepan, combine butter, brown sugar, honey, and golden syrup. Cook over a medium heat until the mixture boils. Add the hot oat mixture, raisins, and banana chips. Mix together.

Line a 25–30cm oblong baking pan with baking paper. Pour mixture into pan and smooth off with a spatula. Place in oven at 200˚C, reduce heat to 170˚C and bake for 15 minutes.

Cool completely, then cut into bars.

"I have to exercise in the morning before my brain figures out what I'm doing"
Marsha Doble

Apricot and Ginger Slice

Heather Heather

250g round wine biscuits
½ cup walnuts
½ cup apricots
½ cup desiccated coconut
⅓ cup crystallised ginger
1 tsp vanilla essence
100g butter
½ cup sweetened condensed milk

In a mixing bowl, combine crushed biscuits, chopped walnuts, apricots, ginger, coconut, and vanilla essence. Melt butter and condensed milk in saucepan over a low heat. Stir into the biscuit mixture. Press into the baking dish and refrigerate for at least one hour.

Ice with lemon icing and garnish with swirls of grated lemon rind.

Upside-down (Maklouba) with Cauliflower

Sosek Shasha

Maklouba, translates as upside-down. This particular dish is a favourite in our house-hold, it is delicious. It also reminds me of family gatherings, especially over weekends, when our family got together with our extended family. You can use either cauliflower or eggplant. This is one of the most versatile dishes in Middle Eastern cuisine, particularly Iraqi cuisine; however, it is also common in Lebanese, Jordanian, Syrian, and Palestinian kitchens. Try this delicious dish with 'Sahtane wa hana' which translates as 'health and prosperity'.

1 kg lamb shoulder
1 medium cauliflower
2 cups rice
½ tsp salt
½ tsp pepper
½ tsp cinnamon
1 tbsp allspice
½ cup butter

Soak the rice in hot water. Cut the lamb into 2-3cm cubes, place in a pot and cover with boiling water. Cook covered for 30 minutes. In a skillet; cut the cauliflower into large florets, or if you prefer, sliced eggplant, fry in butter until golden brown on both sides. Drain the lamb, reserving the broth and, wash the pot to reuse. Put the lamb into the bottom of the pot and sprinkle with half the seasonings. Arrange the fried cauliflower/egg plant on top of the lamb and sprinkle with the remaining seasonings. Next, spread the drained rice on top of the cauliflower. Pour over 3 cups of the reserved lamb broth (add water if necessary). Cook covered, over a low heat until almost dry. Invert the pot and un-mould the Maklouba on a large serving platter. Pour melted butter over the Maklouba, if desired. Serve with a side dish of yoghurt.

Creamy Spinach Dip

Heather Heather

1 tbsp olive oil
250g fresh or frozen spinach
1 medium red onion
2 rashers bacon
250g cream cheese
1 tbsp chives
¼ cup parmesan cheese
¼ cup drained sun dried tomatoes
1 cob loaf of bread
1 clove garlic
¼ cup olive oil

Heat the olive oil in a pan. Add finely chopped onion, bacon and spinach. Cook until onion is soft and any liquid from the spinach has evaporated. Leave to cool.

Combine the spinach mixture with cream cheese, chives, parmesan cheese, sun-dried tomatoes, and mix well.

Cut a lid on a loaf of cob bread and remove bread from the inside. Re-place with the spinach mixture. Heat through in the oven when required. Cut the bread that has been removed into bite sizes and coat with olive oil and crushed garlic, and dry out on a baking tray when heating the cob.

Serve warm with bread on the side for dipping.

Bitterballen

Carla Porter

30–40 balls

This is a well known appetizer in Holland—the bitterballs are usually served with a glass of ice cold 'genever' or Dutch gin. The original recipe uses veal, however I use beef.

3 tbsp butter
5 tbsp flour
1 cup chicken stock
250g cold cooked beef
1 tbsp parsley
salt and pepper
1 tsp Worcester sauce
oil for deep frying
2 egg whites
½ cup fine dry breadcrumbs
Dijon mustard

Heat the butter in a saucepan, add flour and cook, stirring slowly for 2 minutes. Gradually add stock, stirring constantly until a thick paste is formed. Add shredded cooked beef, parsley, salt, pepper, Worchester sauce, and combine thoroughly. Spread mixture on a plate and refrigerate for 2 hours. Form the mixture into 1 inch balls. Dip the balls in the beaten egg white, then roll in the breadcrumbs. Deep fry a few balls at a time for 2 minutes or until golden. Drain on paper towels.

Serve piping hot on wooden cocktail picks with mustard on the side for dipping.

Polenta Flatbread

2 tbsp yeast
1 cup warm water
4 cups high grade flour
1 cup fine polenta flour
2 tsp salt
2 tsp balsamic vinegar
¼ cup olive oil
1½ cups water
¼ cup olive oil
fresh rosemary
rock salt

Sprinkle yeast over warm water and set aside. Mix flours and salt together. Combine yeast and olive oil and pour into flour. Add vinegar and additional water. Mix well, kneading to form a smooth dough. Set aside in an oiled bowl to double in size.

Punch down dough, roll into a rough circle shape and place on greased, floured baking tray.

Brush with olive oil, sprinkle liberally with fresh rosemary leaves and rock salt. Bake for 20 minutes in preheated oven at 180°C.

Wild Venison Loin with Chestnuts

1 kg venison loin
2 tbsp American mustard
1 tbsp Worcester sauce
salt
pepper
600g chestnuts
300g chorizo sausages
oil
1 roll puff pastry
egg wash

Season trimmed venison loin with mustard, Worchester sauce, salt and pepper. Sear all sides in a very hot pan. Refrigerate. Cut a slant into the chestnuts and roast in the oven until soft. Peel immediately and chop finely. Mix the chestnuts with raw chorizo sausage meat and refrigerate. Spread the chestnut mix in a thin layer on sheet of cling-film; place the venison on top and roll up tightly like a sausage roll and refrigerate. Brush puff pastry with egg wash, remove the cling-film from the venison and place on the puff pastry; wrap tightly. Place on a baking tray and brush pastry with egg wash.

Preheat the oven to 240°C, place the venison in oven and reduce temperature to 180°C, bake for 20–25 minutes.

Remove from oven and allow to rest for 5 minutes before slicing.

Timmie's Chorizo Risotto

Tim Beveridge
Singer, Promoter

2–3 tbsp olive oil
(substitute with butter if you like)
2 cups of good quality risotto rice
1 ltr chicken stock—heated
a few threads or a pinch of saffron
2–3 cloves garlic
an onion—red if you like but doesn't really matter
a good glug of white wine
2–3 New Zealand made chorizo, chopped
(it is optional to fry beforehand to reduce fat content)
a cup or so of cooked peas—optional
fresh thyme—also optional but preferred
parmesan cheese

Steep the saffron in a little boiled water and let sit.

"Soffritto"—or fry the chopped garlic and onion in 2–3 tbsp olive oil on a medium/slow heat until soft and clear.
Strip a few branches of thyme to add to the onion and garlic while they are softening.

Add rice and toast it up a little with the soffritto for a minute or two.
Glug in the white wine ttssshh! and reduce.

Add the stock all at once—(don't fluff around with the little by little nonsense).
Add chorizo at some stage—the earlier the better for the spiciness.
Stick the lid on and leave on a low simmering heat.

Part way through (or early as you like) add saffron liquid.
When stock almost all absorbed—give it a good thrashing stir—'mantecare'—to release starches and make it creamy.

Season to taste if necessary.
Stir in a handful of grated parmesan a part of the thrashing—add peas as well.

Serve garnished with a little stripped thyme, parmesan and cracked pepper.

DONE!

Wild Pork in Cider Sauce

4 pork chops
salt
pepper
flour
oil
1 tbsp butter
1 apple
2 tbsp brandy
1 cup apple cider
200ml cream
fresh thyme

Make several small cuts in the pork rind to stop it from curling as it cooks. Season the chops with salt and pepper and coat with flour shaking off the excess. Cook in a medium hot pan for 4–5 minutes each side. Remove from the pan and set aside to rest, keep warm. Peel the apple and cut into wedges. Melt the butter in the pan and add the apple wedges, toss gently for 1–2 minutes, pour in the brandy, cider, cream and finely chopped thyme leaves.

Simmer for 4–5 minutes so the sauce slightly thickens.
Remove from the heat, add the pork chops and the released juices.

Braised Hare in Port with Bacon

1 medium hare (or 1 large rabbit)
salt
pepper
oil
2 onions
5 cloves garlic
250g streaky bacon
2 bay leaves
1 tin chopped tomatoes
250ml port
500ml red wine
500ml chicken stock
3 tbsp plum jam
1 tbsp mustard
3 juniper berries
1 tbsp chopped fresh thyme

Chop up hare into medium-sized pieces, season, and brown in hot oil. Add the onions and bacon, sauté for 5 minutes and add remaining ingredients. Simmer in the oven at 160°C or a crock-pot for approximately one hour or until the meat is tender.

Polenta, mashed potatoes or spaetzle go well as a side dish.

Green Tea and Manuka Smoked Salmon

4 salmon cutlets
  (skin removed)
1 tbsp salt
1 tbsp brown sugar
1 tbsp green tea leaves
2 tbsp manuka sawdust

Rub the salmon with the sugar and salt. Place in fridge for 2–3 hours. Line a heavy skillet with aluminium foil. Moisten tea leaves with a little water and put, with the sawdust, into the skillet. Place a cake rack on top and cover with aluminium foil or lid. Put the skillet onto the stove top on a high heat until the sawdust and tea leaves start to smoke. Alternatively use a barbecue with a lid or wok. Place the salmon on the cake rack, and cover. Reduce to a low heat and smoke until the salmon is just pink inside, approximately 15 minutes.

Serve warm on sticky rice with a wasabi cream (see recipe below) and baby green leaves.

Wasabi Cream

200ml fresh cream
wasabi to taste
juice of ½ lemon

Whisk the cream to very soft peaks, add the wasabi—be careful it can be very hot. Add lemon juice.

Norwegian Fish Layer

Tricia Vickers

1 cup rice
50g butter
2 tbsp flour
1 cup milk
1 tbsp curry powder
1 large can salmon
½ cup chutney
  (tamarillo is the best)
1 cup soft breadcrumbs

Rinse rice in cold water and cook in boiling salted water until tender. Drain. Make a roux sauce using 25g butter, curry powder, flour and milk. Add the salmon. In an ovenproof dish, layer rice, fish sauce and chutney (usually 2 layers of each) finishing with rice on top.
Melt remaining butter and add the bread crumbs.
Sprinkle the buttered breadcrumbs on top.

Bake at 190°C for 30 minutes.

Hokkien Noodles with Prawns

Serves 3-4

400g Hokkien noodles
100g carrots julienne
100g spinach julienne
100g baby broccoli florets
2 tsp sesame oil
1 tbsp shredded ginger
2 tbsp oyster sauce
2 tbsp sweet chilli sauce
12 peeled prawns
zest of ½ lemon

Place noodles in a bowl and cover with boiling water. Allow to stand for two minutes, then drain. Blanch the vegetables in boiling water quickly. Heat oil in a wok or frying pan, add all the ingredients except the noodles, cook for 2–3 minutes.

Add noodles and cook for a further 2–3 minutes until noodles have heated through.

Oven Baked Snapper

1 tbsp butter
2 small snapper
salt
pepper
400ml coconut cream
200ml fresh cream
2 tbsp fish sauce
1 red capsicum
1 yellow capsicum
400g button mushrooms
2 limes
2 red chillies
mint leaves for garnish

Grease with butter, an oblong oven-proof dish large enough to fit both fish lying flat. Scour the skin of the snapper and season liberally with salt and pepper and place in dish. Cut the capsicums into 1cm pieces, halve button mushrooms and limes, finely chop the de-seeded chilli and arrange on top of the fish. Mix together the coconut cream, fresh cream, fish sauce and pour over.

Cover with aluminium foil and bake at 170˚C until cooked, approximately 50-60 minutes depending on the size of the fish.

Just before serving, sprinkle with finely sliced mint leaves.

Eggplant Caponata

This is a traditional Sicilian eggplant dish that is great served up as a dip accompanied by different breads or crackers, spread on a pizza base topped with feta, or as condiment with cold meats.

1 cup olive oil
1 large eggplant
1 onion
½ celery stick
2 tbsp tomato paste
6 tbsp balsamic vinegar
½ can chopped tomatoes
1 tbsp raw sugar
3 squares 70% cocoa chocolate
4 tbsp pitted black olives
3 tbsp small capers
2 tbsp pine nuts
1 tbsp basil
salt
ground pepper

Peel and dice the eggplant into 1cm cubes. Fry in a skillet with the olive oil on a high heat until golden, 3–4 minutes. Using a slotted spoon remove the eggplant from the skillet and set aside. Sauté the finely diced onion and celery in the remaining oil until golden. Add tomato paste and cook, stirring, for a further 1–2 minutes. Add the balsamic vinegar, tinned tomatoes and sugar, bring to the boil, then add the chocolate and remove from the heat. While still warm: combine the eggplant, onion and tomato mix, with coarsely chopped black olives, well rinsed and dried capers, pine nuts and chopped basil. Season with salt and pepper.

Best served at room temperature.

"The secret of getting ahead is getting started"
Mark Twain

Anchovy Twists

Mary Mathis

Makes 20

50g anchovies
3 tbsp parmesan cheese
¾ cup grated cheese
1 sheet puff pastry
1 egg

Finely chop the anchovy's and mix with some of the oil, the parmesan and grated cheeses. Brush the pastry with the beaten egg. Spread the filling over the pastry and cover with cling-film. Press the filling into the pastry using a rolling pin. Fold the pastry in half, cut into 1cm wide strips and slice off the folded edge. Unfold the strips and twist, place on a lined baking tray. Fan bake at 200°C for about 10 minutes until golden brown. Can be served hot or cold.

Savoury Chicken Cheesecake

Goldie Argent

Serves 8–10

Base:
125g plain biscuits
2 tsp mixed herbs
90g melted butter

Mix together crushed biscuits and other ingredients and spread over a greased 25cm spring-form tin.

Filling:
250g cream cheese
3 egg yolks
⅓ cup cream
30g butter
1 medium onion
2 tbsp plain flour
⅔ cup chicken stock
90g grated mature cheese
1 tsp dry mustard
salt
pepper
½ cup chopped ham
2 cups cooked chicken
3 egg whites

In a small bowl beat the softened cream cheese until smooth. Beat in egg yolks and cream. Sauté onions in butter until soft. Stir in flour and gradually blend in stock, and simmer until thickened. Stir in cheese, mustard, pepper, and salt to taste. Add cream cheese mixture, chopped ham and chicken. Beat egg whites to soft peaks and fold in gently. Pour over base and bake 1–1½ hours at 90˚C until golden and firm.

Put the cheesecake on a platter, top with mushroom sauce (see below), and sprinkle with parsley.

Mushroom Sauce

Goldie Argent

2 tbsp butter
6 medium/large mushrooms
2 tbsp cream
60g mature cheese
parsley

Sauté mushrooms until soft. Add cream and cheese and heat until melted.

Chicken Casserole

Heather Heather

4 chicken legs
2 carrots
1 red onion
½ cup white wine
2 tbsp tomato sauce
1 tsp chicken stock powder
2 tbsp soy sauce
3 tsp brown sugar
2 tbsp cornflour
450g pineapple pieces
450g mushrooms
salt
pepper

Place the chicken legs, finely chopped carrots, and onion in casserole dish. Combine the rest of the ingredients and pour over. Cook in a moderate oven for two hours.

Half an hour before serving, add the pineapple pieces and chopped mushrooms.

Shanghai Sweet and Sour Pork

Lyn Hughes

When my mother-in-law was expatriated from Shanghai to NZ at the beginning of WW2, she and her very good friend (also expatriated from Shanghai) got together. They spent many hours trying to recreate their favourite dish that her cook would make in Shanghai. This is what they came up with and the recipe is written in the way it has been passed on to me—it is simple and a Hughes family favourite.

cook pork pieces (2lb for 7 minutes in a pressure cooker)
bring to boil 2 tbsp golden syrup
2 tbsp vinegar
2 tbsp tomato sauce
¼ cup vinegar
½ cup pork stock
1 tsp crushed ginger
add pork pieces

Gently simmer for 15 minutes. Thicken with corn flour. Serve on rice.

Cocktail Meatballs with Homemade Chutney

Heather Heather

500g steak mince
½ cup fresh breadcrumbs
¼ cup milk
½ cup coconut
1 small red onion
1 egg
1 tsp Worcester sauce
salt
pepper

Combine all the ingredients together and shape into small balls. Cook in the microwave.

Chutney Sauce:
½ cup tomato sauce
½ cup plum jam
2 tbsp orange juice
2 tsp mustard
salt
pepper

Mix all the ingredients together and cook in the microwave for 2 minutes.

Stir in the cooked meatballs, serve with cocktail sticks on the side.

Bean Salad

Judy Keaney,
Former Mayoress of Rotorua

This recipe makes a large salad and was given to me by my friend of 66 years. For all of our primary schooling we walked to and from school every day except when it was raining. The friendship has endured.

Salad Ingredients:
1 cup cooked brown rice
½ cup sultanas
½ cup currants
2 cans of mixed beans
¼ cup poppy seeds
¼ cup toasted sesame seeds
4 stalks celery
2 red or green peppers
handful chopped parsley
¾ cup roasted peanuts

Dressing:
½ cup oil
1 tsp curry powder
½ cup vinegar

Dressing: heat the oil, add curry powder and "sizzle" for no more than a minute. Remove from the heat and slowly pour in vinegar (it splutters, so take care). Bring to the boil and simmer for 5 minutes. Allow to cool.

Place all the salad ingredients in a large bowl, pour over the cooled dressing, just before serving add roasted peanuts.

Autumn is a time of harvest,
of gathering together......
Anonymous

Cucumber & Potato Salad

This salad originates from Austria—it's a favourite of ours, easy to make and always popular.

1 telegraph cucumber
3 medium potatoes
250g sour cream
100g plain yogurt
1 clove garlic
1 tsp caraway seed
cider vinegar to taste
salt
white pepper

Boil the potatoes in their jacket, then peel and slice very thinly. Peel cucumber and slice thinly. Finely chop garlic together with caraway seeds. Mix all ingredients together just before serving. If you are not a fan of caraway, try replacing it with fresh dill.

Tamarillo Chutney

Tricia Vickers

1 kg tamarillos
300g cooking apples
300g onions
1½ tsp salt
½ tsp cayenne pepper
120g raisins (or sultanas)
400g brown sugar
300ml vinegar
½ tsp whole allspice
¼ tsp peppercorns
¼ tsp whole cloves
2 dried chillies

Skin and chop tamarillos. Peel, core and dice the apples. Peel and chop onions. Combine tamarillos, apples, onions, salt, cayenne, raisins (chopped if large), brown sugar and vinegar in a large saucepan. Tie spices in a piece of muslin or clean cotton and add to saucepan. Simmer gently for 1–1½ hours until thick.

Pour into warm jars and seal.

Red Wine Marinated Tamarillos

Kirstine Jolly

8 tamarillos
½ cup red wine
½ cup orange juice
1 cup sugar

Boil the tamarillos for a few minutes until skins are easily removed. Remove skins and leave the stalks intact. Make up a marinade with red wine, orange juice and sugar. Put marinade into a plastic container and add tamarillos. Marinate for several hours (the longer the better—they can keep until the following day). Gently move the tamarillos within the marinade several times, so they are coated and thoroughly flavoured.

Serve with ice cream!

winter

Winter Food

Smoked Paprika Beef Soup

Kirstine Jolly

This tasty, easy recipe has evolved over time as a result of needing to use up large quantities of homegrown beef, it is easy and tasty. It should be cooked slowly in a crock-pot, the long slow cooking process means that it's great for using up inexpensive beef cuts. The ingredients can be varied and the quantities are not prescriptive. It needs at least 5 hours cooking time. Serve with fresh, crunchy French bread.

½–1kg of cubed beef
oil
2 chorizo sausages
1–2 onions
2–3 cloves garlic
1 tsp of hot-smoked paprika
(this secret ingredient is a must!)
one carton of real beef stock
assorted root vegetables:
carrot, potato, kumara
1 tub of tomato paste
1 can of tomatoes or
fresh peeled tomatoes
1 can of kidney beans
salt and pepper

Turn a frying pan on high and quickly brown the beef in oil that has a high burn point (rice bran oil is good). Do not cook the beef! Place the browned beef in the crock-pot and gently fry the chorizo sausages, onions, garlic and smoked paprika in the frying pan. Add these to the crock-pot. Place all the other ingredients in the crock-pot and, if possible let it cook for the whole day, on medium if possible, or 5 hours on high.

Optional; At the end you can add cooked pasta or lightly sautéed mushrooms. You may replace the kidney beans with cannellini beans.

Tasty Mince Pinwheels

Carla Porter

500g sausage meat
2 tsp sweet chutney or relish
½ tsp curry powder
1 green apple peeled and grated
1 onion finely chopped
375g puff pastry
1 egg white

Combine mince, chutney, curry powder, apple, and onion in a bowl. Roll out half the pastry on a lightly floured surface to 30cm square. Spread half the mix over the pastry leaving a 2.5cm border around the edge. Roll up like a Swiss roll, brush with egg white. Using a serrated knife cut the roll into 1cm slices. Repeat with remaining pastry and mince mixture.

Place pinwheels on oven tray, bake at 180°C for 20 minutes or until golden.

Savoury Pumpkin Streusel Torte

½ kg onions
4 cloves garlic
½ kg cubed pumpkin
olive oil
2 cups flour
8 tsp baking powder
pinch of chilli powder
¼ tsp salt
100g melted butter
1 ½ cups natural yogurt

Quickly pan-fry the diced onion and garlic in olive oil until golden. Remove from the pan and pan-fry the cubed pumpkin to caramelise the outside. Cool. Mix all remaining ingredients to batter consistency, fold in the pumpkin and onion. Pour into a greased and floured cake tin.

Top with the Cheese and Herb Streusel (below) and bake at 170°C for 60 minutes.

Cheese and Herb Streusel

100g flour
100g butter
200g tasty cheese
200g cottage cheese
1 tsp chopped rosemary
1 tsp chopped thyme
1 tsp chopped parsley
¼ tsp cracked pepper

Mix all ingredients together to form a crumble. Use topping for Savoury Pumpkin Streusel Torte.

Mama's Potato Soup

1. Always remember Mum's Birthday.
2. Always remember to call Mum on Valentine's Day.
3. Remember to ring and tell her what a wonderful cook she is (often).
4. Remember to tell her that nobody else's Potato Soup is anywhere near as good as hers.
5. Remember to tell her in advance when you will be picking up the pot of yummy soup.
6. Remember to include chocolate or flowers when you return the empty pot.
7. In case your Mum's Potato Soup is not that nice here is my Mum's …...

800g potatoes
1.5 ltr chicken stock
1 onion
2 cloves of garlic
2 bay leaves
50g butter
10g flour
salt
white pepper
sour cream
bacon and thyme to garnish

Dice the peeled potatoes into 2cm cubes. Place in a large pot with chicken stock and bay leaves. Bring to the boil and cook until potatoes are just soft. In a pan, heat the butter, add flour, and roast until it is a dark golden colour. Add the flour butter/mixture to the soup and boil for 4–5 minutes.

Serve with fried bacon strips, sour cream and fresh thyme.

Pumpkin Soup

Pumpkin soup is always a winter-warming meal and children of all ages seem to love it. This is the basic recipe but you can jazz it up by adding coconut cream at the end, or by serving it with a bowl of grated cheese and diced, fried bacon.

2 carrots
2 cloves garlic
1 onion
oil
1 kg pumpkin
2 tbsp tomato paste
2 tsp curry powder
1 tsp cumin
½ tsp nutmeg
2 tbsp smoked paprika
chicken or vegetable stock

In a large saucepan, sauté finely chopped onions, garlic, and diced carrots. Add diced pumpkin, tomato paste and spices. Sauté a further 2–3 minutes. Add the chicken stock to just cover the vegetables. Simmer until the pumpkin is cooked. Puree until smooth. Season with salt and pepper to taste.
Serve with a dollop of sour cream and croutons or fresh bread.

Bok Choy with Sesame Glaze

2 tbsp sesame oil
4 tbsp sesame seeds
2 garlic cloves
1 tbsp honey
2 tbsp soy sauce
1 cup vegetable stock
juice of 1 lemon
½ tsp cornflour
6 baby bok choy

To make the glaze, lightly toast sesame seeds in sesame oil. Add garlic, honey, soy sauce, vegetable stock, and lemon juice. Bring to the boil and thicken with cornflour.

Cut bok choy in half and boil in salted water. Drain well and serve with the Sesame Glaze.

Lentil and Bacon Cottage Pie

250g brown lentils
2 onions
5 cloves garlic
400g bacon
2 carrots
2 celery sticks
2 x 400g cans tomatoes
2 bay leaves
1 tbsp mild chilli powder
salt
pepper
mashed potatoes
cheddar cheese

Boil lentils in unsalted water until soft (cooking dried pulses in unsalted water makes them rehydrate and soften faster). Brown the diced onions in oil, add diced bacon, carrots, celery, garlic, tomatoes, and the rest of the ingredients including the drained lentils. Simmer for 10–15 minutes. Pour into an oven proof serving dish, top with mashed potatoes and tasty cheddar, brown under the grill.

Jenny's Tandoori Chicken

Jenny Eaves

This recipe uses saffron threads, but if you can't access these or they are too expensive, try without.

1 tsp saffron threads
2½ tbsp boiling water
8–10 chicken drumsticks or
6 larger pieces
6 tbsp lemon juice
3 tsp salt
1½ tsp coriander seeds
1 tsp cumin seeds
5cm fresh root ginger
3 cloves garlic
250ml natural yoghurt
¼–½ tsp cayenne pepper
red food colouring
4 tsp butter, margarine or ghee

Drop saffron threads into a small bowl. Pour over boiling water and soak for 5 minutes. Pat the chicken dry and place in a baking dish in one layer. Mix together lemon juice and salt and rub over the chicken. Pour over the saffron—and the water it has been soaking in—and marinate at room temperature for 30 minutes. Sprinkle coriander and cumin seeds into a small, ungreased frying-pan and toast over a moderate heat for a minute, shaking the pan constantly. Place the toasted seeds, chopped ginger, garlic and 2 tablespoons of yoghurt in a blender and blend at high speed to a smooth paste. Scrape paste into a bowl, add remaining yoghurt, cayenne pepper to taste and enough red food colouring to produce a deep pink colour.

Spread the mixture evenly over the chicken pieces, cover the dish and marinate for 24 hours in the refrigerator. Preheat oven to 200°C. Place a small knob of butter/margarine/ghee on each chicken piece. Roast uncovered for 15 minutes. Reduce heat to 165°C and cook for a further 30–40 minutes, basting 2–3 times.

Tandoori chicken is delicious eaten hot or cold.

TīTī with Watercress and Kumara

Wayne (Buck) Shelford
Former All Black Captain, Rugby Legend

He kai reka!
I love tītī as a kai, it's different and a real delicacy. Our Dad used to just boil it for hours in a traditional way. This recipe is an upmarket slant. Growing up in Rotorua was great with plenty to do for us kids, hanging out with our mates, riding our bikes everywhere, eeling, getting koura and fishing for trout. Good clean fun.
I would like to acknowledge Ann Thorpe from her Kai Ora television series and her book for this wonderful recipe.

2 tītī (mutton birds)
large pot of watercress
6 small kumara
salt and pepper

Bring large pot of water to the boil containing tītī. Simmer for 2 hours, (it smells really strong so leave windows open in kitchen). Turn off the heat, take out tītī and then pour off some of the stock. Replace with hot water to same amount and put in kumara and watercress. Simmer until cooked. Meanwhile preheat the grill until hot, place tītī in a roasting dish under grill for about 10 minutes until skin crisps up. Place watercress on a plate and kumara on the side. Break tītī up and place on watercress. Season and serve.

Southern Pork Casserole

Coral Day

4 pork chops
flour
salt
pepper
oil
1 large onion
2 cloves garlic
4 medium potatoes
1 large cooking apple
1 medium can tomatoes
2 tbsp brown sugar
1 large tbsp mustard

Lightly coat the meat with seasoned flour and brown in a pan of hot oil. Remove the meat from the pan and set aside. Place the potatoes, peeled and sliced thickly, on the base of a casserole dish. Put meat on top. Peel the apple and slice thickly, put on top of the meat. In the remaining oil in the pan, brown the sliced onion and chopped garlic. Add the tomatoes, brown sugar and mustard and heat through. Pour the sauce over the contents in the casserole dish and cover with a lid or aluminium foil.

Put in the oven, preheated to 170°C, for 1–1½ hours.

Serve with rice and a coleslaw made with a mustard or lemon and oil dressing.

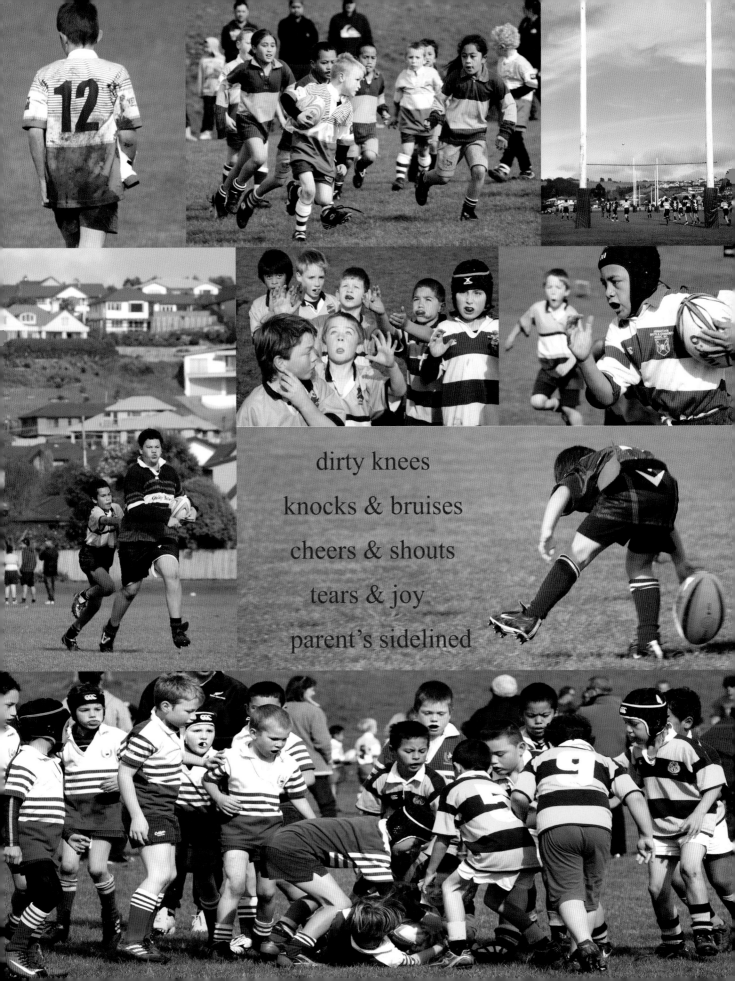

dirty knees

knocks & bruises

cheers & shouts

tears & joy

parent's sidelined

Pakistani Curry

Coral Day

This recipe has always been the family favourite, I originally received it from a friend while living in Singapore in 1965. They, in turn, got it from a Pakistani Army Officer. Time consuming to make so best made a day or two ahead for dinner parties. We used to eat this very hot, but you can adjust the number of chillies used to suit your taste.

500g skirt steak or
gravy beef
1 kg onions
250g butter
small cup of water or stock
2 bay leaves
6 cloves
6 chillies (adjust number for heat)
2 tsp curry powder
1 tsp ground coriander
1 tsp cumin
½ tsp cayenne pepper
½ tsp turmeric
1 clove garlic
1 large can tomatoes
or 500g fresh tomatoes
salt to taste

Melt the butter to boiling point and add sliced onions. Cook until dark brown in colour, stirring often. Once the onions are a rich, dark colour, add the spices (except salt) and sauté for a few minutes. Remove from the heat, add water and diced beef. Return to the heat and cook until juices begin to run, add tomatoes. Cook slowly until tender. Add salt to taste.

Notes; I like to use a crock-pot, but you can cook this in a casserole dish in the oven for approximately 2 hours on 160°C. In order to get the best flavour you must have dark onions (if they start to catch, add a little water). You can also use oil rather than butter. Always keep the ratio of 2–to–1 meat/onions and adjust the seasoning to taste. Serve with rice, naan bread and a selection of small side dishes; cucumber or banana in natural yogurt, coconut, diced tamarillo etc.

Minted Cucumber Yoghurt

This side dish goes well with any curry or other spicy food

2 cups natural yogurt
1 medium sized cucumber
mint
juice of 1 lime

Peel and dice cucumber into medium sized cubes, add lime juice and yoghurt. Sprinkle with finely chopped mint just prior to serving.

Kumara and Pumpkin Curry

Don't be put off by the long list of ingredients—this is an inexpensive and heart-warming meal. It doesn't take long to prepare and the whole family will enjoy it. Serve with rice, poppadoms or naan.

5 tbsp sunflower oil
½ kg onions
3 cloves garlic
1 tsp ground turmeric
2 tsp coriander seeds
2 tsp cardamom seeds
2 tsp ground cumin
2 tsp caraway seeds
1 tsp mild chilli powder
2 tsp mild curry powder
1 tbsp sweet paprika
1 ltr chicken stock
2 bay leaves
8 kaffir lime leaves
1 kg kumara
1 kg pumpkin
salt and pepper to taste

Sauté onions and garlic until golden, then add the spices and gently fry over a low heat. Add the chicken stock, bay leaves and lime leaves (optional), and bring to the boil. Add peeled vegetables cut into medium-sized cubes. Cook for 15–20 minutes or until vegetables are soft.

Naan Bread

2 tsp dry yeast
½ cup warm water
1 cup natural yoghurt
1 cup boiling water
6½ cups flour
2 tbsp vegetable oil
1 tbsp vinegar
2 tsp salt

Pour the warm water into a large bowl, and sprinkle with yeast. Put the yoghurt in a separate bowl, slowly stir in the boiling water. Allow to cool. Stir yoghurt mixture into the yeast mixture. Gradually stir in 3 cups of flour, and continue to stir for 2 minutes. Cover with plastic and allow to stand for 30 minutes. Add oil, vinegar and salt. Mix in remaining flour until a dough is formed. Turn out onto a lightly floured surface and knead until smooth and elastic. Add more flour if the dough becomes too sticky.

Lightly oil the large bowl. Add the dough and turn to ensure the entire surface is coated. Cover with a damp cloth and leave to rise until doubled in volume. Meanwhile, place a pizza stone or baking tray in the centre of the oven and heat to 230°C.

Once the dough has risen. Push the dough down and divide into 6 pieces. Using lightly floured hands, flatten each piece into an oval shape, cover and let rest a further 10 minutes.

Stretch into a long oval shape, lay on heated pizza stone/baking tray, press down firmly. Bake for 10–15 minutes, turning once until the naan is fluffy and brown. Wrap in foil to keep soft until ready to serve.

Chapatti

½ kg wholemeal flour
1 cup water (approx)
salt
melted butter

Mix flour and water and a pinch of salt to a stiff dough. Knead well. Place dough in a bowl, cover and leave in a warm place for 30 minutes. Pinch pieces off the dough and mould them into small balls. Roll each ball in flour and roll them out until no thicker than a pancake. Place chapatti's in an ungreased, hot, heavy-based pan and fry for 2 minutes each side. Brush with melted butter on both sides and fry to a light brown colour.

Potato Bake with Smoked Trout

1 kg of waxy potatoes
500ml cream
pinch of nutmeg
salt
white pepper
1 tbsp butter
3 cloves garlic
2 cups grated cheese
hot-smoked trout

Butter an oven-proof dish and sprinkle with finely chopped garlic. Slice the peeled potatoes into ½ cm thick slices and layer into the dish. Season well and pour over the cream. Cover with aluminium foil and bake at 180˚C for 30 minutes. Remove the foil, sprinkle over the grated cheese and place under the grill to brown.

Top with flaked hot-smoked trout and serve.

Geothermal Trout with Vegetables

Charles P.T. Royal

Serves 4–6

There are a variety of ways to cook and serve vegetables. If you happen to live in Rotorua, you can steam them naturally in a natural geothermal cooking pool or steam box. If you don't have access to geothermal, you can always use a double boiler or steamer pot at home. If you want the flavour of the earth, try smoking them first and then roasting them just before serving. Better still, cook them in a hangi (earth oven).

Talking with local growers at the market is always a way to learn about all sorts of vegetables. The vegetables in this recipe are Kinaki NZ® Ingredients which can be bought from www.maorifood.com, but you can substitute them with locally foraged or home-grown produce.

As trout cannot be purchased from shops or supermarkets in New Zealand, you can use any other fish of your choice in this recipe.

Kinaki NZ® Produce
200g puha sow thistle
200g pikopiko fern shoots
200g urenika Maori potato
200g kumara (sweet potato)
200g pirita supplejack vine
      shoots
200g hākeka ear fungus
200g hārore wood mushrooms
200g pūkurau puff balls

Trout
200g watercress
200g courgettes
200g red onions

Method 1:
Clean trout or the substitute fish and place, with all other produce, onto a tray and cook in a steam box for 40 minutes.
Wrap puha, pikopiko, pirita, urenika and kumara into a clean cloth. Place into the cooking pool for 40 minutes.

Method 2:
Lay cleaned trout, stomach down and fins open, onto a cake rack. Place the rack in a roasting dish (it should be raised off the bottom of the pan) and add 2 cups of hot water. Cover with a lid or aluminium foil and place into a hot oven, preheated to 200°C, for 40 minutes. Wash and place urenika and kumara into the bottom of a double-boiler pot. Cover with cold water. Place all other produce into the top pot (the steam cooker). Sit this on top of the kumara and urenika potato and bring to the boil. Turn the element down and allow to simmer for 40 minutes. Check the urenika and kumara is cooked by testing with a knife, when it is soft but firm, remove from the heat.

Serve vegetables and fish together on a large platter.

Rotorua Mud Cake

This cake has a very different texture. It is dense and richly flavoured, and can be served either warm or cold. Serve with berries and/or crème anglaise. The Rotorua Mud Cake was a favourite when we had The Great Dessert Company in Auckland – it sold from high end restaurants to airline caterers.

250g butter
250g cooking chocolate
100g caster sugar
80g brown sugar
400g hot water
20g coffee
185g self raising flour
23g cocoa powder
2 eggs
1 tbsp vanilla essence

In a large mixing bowl put the melted butter, melted chocolate, caster sugar, brown sugar, hot water, and coffee. Mix well until smooth. Sieve together flour and cocoa. Add to the chocolate mix, the eggs and vanilla, beat until combined. Fold in flour and cocoa.

Pour into a greased 23cm cake tin and bake at 150°C for approximately 50 minutes.

Apple Caramel Upside-down Cake

Topping:
100g butter
4 large apples
1 lemon
250g caster sugar
1 tsp vanilla

Cake:
100g butter
200g caster sugar
4 egg yolks
6 egg whites
1 tsp vanilla
200g flour
¼ tsp salt
2 tsp baking powder
1 tsp cinnamon

Peel and core the apples, slice into 1cm thick wedges. Toss in the juice and zest of 1 lemon. Melt butter in large pan, add the apples and cook for 3 minutes. Add the sugar and vanilla and cook for another 5 minutes. Remove the apples from the pan with a slotted spoon and arrange on the bottom of a greased, lined 23cm cake tin. Increase the heat under the pan and boil the liquid to a light caramel colour—the caramel will continue to colour once you remove from the heat so be careful not to over caramelise the sauce. Pour the caramel over the apples in the cake tin.

Cream the butter and sugar until light and fluffy, slowly add egg yolks and vanilla. Sieve together the flour, baking powder, salt, and cinnamon. Fold the flour into the creamed butter. Whisk egg whites until stiff and fold through the cake mix. Spread on top of apples and bake at 160°C for approximately 45 minutes.

Allow the cake to cool slightly before removing from the tin.

Pumpkin Cake

125g butter
1¼ cups sugar
2 eggs
1 cup mashed cooked pumpkin
⅓ cup milk
⅓ cup sour cream
1¾ cups flour
½ cup
2 tsp baking powder
1 tsp soda
1 tsp salt
2 tsp cinnamon
½ tsp nutmeg
¾ cup chocolate chips
¾ cup chopped walnuts

Cream the butter and sugar. Add eggs slowly, beating well. In a separate bowl, combine pumpkin, milk and sour cream. In another bowl, sift together the dry ingredients. Fold the dry ingredients into the butter mixture, alternately with the pumpkin mixture. Add the chocolate and nuts.

Bake at 180°C for 50–60 minutes.

Lemon, Lime and Poppyseed Syrup Cake

125g unsalted butter
2 tsp finely grated lemon zest
2 tsp finely grated lime zest
1¼ cups of caster sugar
3 eggs
1½ cups of flour
2 tsp baking powder
2 tbsp poppyseeds
100ml plain yoghurt

Syrup:
3 tbsp lime juice
3 tbsp lemon juice
3 tbsp caster sugar

Preheat the oven to 180°C and prepare a 23cm cake tin. Beat the butter, lime and lemon zest until light and fluffy. Gradually add sugar continuously beating until well mixed and creamy. Add eggs, one at a time, beating well. Combine the flour, baking powder and poppy seeds; fold into the butter mixture, alternating with the yoghurt. Pour into the prepared cake tin and bake for 30–35 minutes.

Allow to cool for 3–5 minutes before turning out of the tin.

To make the syrup: place the lime and lemon juice and sugar in a pan, simmer gently, stirring until the sugar has dissolved. Bring to the boil and boil for 3 minutes without stirring. Pour the hot syrup over the warm cake. Serve warm as a dessert with crème fraiche or cold as a tea cake with softly whipped cream.

Chocolate and Banana Cake

Carla Porter

Delicious and easy!

1½ cups self raising flour
255g soft butter
1 cup caster sugar
2 tsp baking powder
4 eggs
6ml (¼ cup) milk
200g dark chocolate (chopped)
2 large ripe bananas

Chocolate Frosting:
450g icing sugar
80g cocoa
150g melted butter
5 tbsp milk

Beat together the flour, butter, sugar, baking powder and eggs until well combined. Beat in milk. Use a metal spoon to fold in the chocolate and bananas. Pour the mixture into a greased and lined medium sized cake tin. Bake for approx 40 minutes at 180˚C.

Leave the cake to cool before making the frosting.

Sift sugar and cocoa into a bowl. Add the melted butter and milk and beat until thick. Cut the cake into 3 layers and spread each layer with frosting.

Decorate with berries.

"When it comes to chocolate ....resistance is futile!"
Anonymous

Connie's Fudge Cake

Jenny Eaves

This was a recipe of my mother's, I usually make a double quantity. Nuts and dried fruit may also be added if you wish.

125g butter
125g sugar
1 egg
2 tsp cocoa
vanilla
250g wine or malt biscuits

Melt butter and sugar. Stir in beaten egg and cocoa. Bring just to the boil. Remove from the heat, add crushed biscuits and vanilla. Pour into a tin lined with greased paper and pat down the mixture so that it spreads evenly across the bottom of the pan.

Ice with chocolate icing and refrigerate.

Date Cake

Cheryl O'Connell

1 cup dates
1 cup hot water
1 tsp baking soda
125g butter
1 cup sugar
1 tsp vanilla essence
pinch of salt
1 egg, beaten
1 cup high grade flour
1 tsp baking powder

Topping:
50g butter
1 cup coconut
1 tbsp milk
1 cup brown sugar

Boil the dates and baking soda in the hot water for 3 minutes. Add butter and sugar, and stir until the sugar has melted. Leave to cool. Add vanilla essence, salt and egg. Stir gently to combine. Fold in flour and baking powder. Pour into greased and floured cake tin (the mixture is very moist) and bake at 180°C for approximately 20 minutes.

Topping: bring the butter, coconut, milk and brown sugar to a simmer and stir until dissolved.

Remove the cake from oven when it's almost cooked, and coat with the topping before returning it to the oven for a further 8–10 minutes.

Serve as a dessert with Greek yogurt.

Feijoa Loaf

Rosie Waller

8 feijoas
1 cup sugar
60g butter
1 cup boiling water
2 cups flour
1 tsp baking powder
1 tsp baking soda
pinch of salt
1 egg
4 tsp of ginger

Place the peeled and chopped feijoas, sugar, butter and boiling water in a pot, and bring to the boil and simmer for 5 minutes. Let the mixture cool. Carefully fold in the dry ingredients and then the beaten egg. Stir briskly but don't over beat. Lastly fold in the ginger.

Grease and flour a loaf tin, pour in the mixture and bake at 180˚C for 50–60 minutes.

Let stand in the tin for 5–10 minutes before turning out.

Feijoa Chutney

800g feijoas
200g apples
1½ cups raw sugar
1 cup cider vinegar
¼ tsp chilli powder

Peel and dice the feijoas and apples. Boil together, all ingredients in a heavy-bottomed saucepan until thick, 30–60 minutes.

Bottle into sterilised jars.

Persimmon Chutney

1 kg persimmons
1 lemon
½ tsp salt
1½ cups sugar
1 tsp chilli sauce
2 tbsp finely chopped ginger
3 cloves chopped garlic
1 cup malt vinegar

Blanch the persimmons, in boiling water for 3 minutes. Drain and stand under cold running water before peeling and dicing into small cubes. Place the diced persimmon, whole diced lemon and all other ingredients into a heavy saucepan and bring to the boil. Boil gently, stirring frequently, for a further 60 minutes or until the mixture is thick. Remove from the stove. While still hot, pour into hot sterilised jars, and seal.

Persimmon Jelly

1½ kilos persimmons
2 cups water
juice of 1 lemon
1 packet of pectin
1 cup honey

Place peeled and cut persimmons into a heavy saucepan and cover with water. Bring to the boil and, once cooked, mash. Reduce the heat and allow to simmer for a further 10 minutes. Remove from the heat. Push the fruit pulp through a strainer. Using 3 cups of the strained pulp, stir in lemon juice and pectin. Bring to the boil and add honey. Keep at a full rolling boil for 1–2 minutes, stirring constantly. Pour into hot, sterilised jars and cover.

smokefree

NO SMOKING

auahi kore

Thermal Activity

+ Fresh Fruit &

Vege

+ Rewena Bread

+ Bric a Brac

+ Saturday Morning

Gossip

= Kuirau Park Flea

Market

Aunty Doa's

Fresh

REWENA

BREAD

Roast Vegetable Salad

Joanne Bryant

Serves 4

2 medium kumara
½ medium pumpkin
2 carrots
2 parsnips
1 fresh red pepper
  (or roasted peppers in a jar)
olive oil
2–4 cloves garlic
fresh rosemary leaves chopped.
salt
ground black pepper
handful green beans
balsamic vinegar
aioli

Cut the kumara and pumpkin into wedges, and the peeled carrots and parsnips into batons. Place kumara, pumpkin, carrots, parsnips and red pepper (if fresh), in a large roasting dish with olive oil, garlic, rosemary, salt and pepper. Roast in a single layer at 220˚C for 35–40 minutes until brown and crisp. If using peppers from a jar, add just before removing from the oven to lightly brown. Lastly add cooked beans to the roasting dish. Remove from the oven and drizzle with balsamic vinegar. You may serve this either warm or at room temperature, drizzled with Aioli Dressing (see recipe below).

Aioli

4 egg yolks
1 tbsp cider vinegar
2 tbsp Dijon mustard
1 tbsp Worcester Sauce
6 cloves garlic
salt
white pepper
500ml sunflower oil
lemon juice to taste

Blend in food processor, egg yolks, garlic, vinegar, mustard, Worcester sauce, salt and pepper. With processor on high, very slowly pour in oil to achieve a mayonnaise style sauce.

Add lemon juice to taste.

Citrus Kumara Salad

1 kg kumara
2 tbsp oil
½ kg oranges
salt
white pepper
1 spring onion
3 mild, de-seeded red chillies
5 tbsp toasted sunflower seeds

Peel oranges and fillet out segments Squeeze the remaining orange and place juice to one side. Cut the peeled kumara into medium-sized wedges; season with salt and pepper, and drizzle with oil. Roast in oven at 200°C until golden. Remove from the oven and drizzle with orange juice while still hot.

Arrange the orange fillets and kumara on a platter, coat with Lime and Honey Dressing (see below), and garnish with the finely sliced spring onion and chillies. Sprinkle with sunflower seeds.

Lime and Honey Dressing

1 tbsp liquid honey
40ml lime or lemon juice
50ml good quality sunflower oil

Mix together all ingredients. Stir until the honey is dissolved.

Tante Janny's Hot Beetroot

Mere Marshall

Tante Janny's Hot Beetroot is a family recipe from my husband, Martin Tissink's family. It is a firm favourite with my immediate and extended whanau. We have a large Dutch community, with the supported immigration programme at the end of 1950s and 1960s significantly contributing to the number of Dutch people who have made New Zealand their home. I noticed last time I was at the Rotorua Netherlands Hall they served a lovely salad incorporating beetroot in large amounts—delicious. A well liked vegetable I think.

1 tbsp oil
1 onion
2 cloves garlic
200g bacon pieces
1 cup grated apple
1 tsp mace
1 tsp nutmeg
1 tsp ginger
1 tsp paprika
½ tsp cayenne
1 tbsp grainy mustard
5 cups cooked and grated
or small cubed beetroot
2 tbsp cider vinegar
1 tsp brown sugar (optional)

Heat the oil in a wide, heavy-based saucepan. Sauté the chopped onions and crushed garlic, add the bacon pieces and cook until crisp. Add grated apple, mustard and spices, mix well. Next add the beetroot, vinegar and sugar. Stir to combine. Simmer for approximately 10–15 minutes, stirring often to avoid burning. Add water a little at a time if the mixture becomes to dry.

I serve this with potatoes and a green salad, or broccoli sprinkled with parmesan.

Beet and Carrot Salad

Britta Noske

¼ cup extra virgin olive oil
2 tbsp cider vinegar or lemon juice
salt
pepper
3 cups grated raw beetroot
3 cups grated raw carrot
1 cup torn flat-leaf parsley
½ cups snipped chives
¼ cup sunflower seeds

In a bowl, place olive oil, vinegar, salt and pepper and whisk to combine. Add the beetroot and carrot, toss thoroughly, and set aside at room temperature for about 10 minutes—tossing occasionally. The carrot will pick up the beetroot colour and the dressing soaks in. Add the sunflower seeds, and parsley, toss again.

Sprinkle with chives and serve.

Roast Chicken with Mushroom Stuffing

1 medium chicken
salt
pepper
oil
water

Dry the chicken with a paper towel. With wet hands, firmly press the prepared stuffing into the stomach cavity, close the opening with skewers so the stuffing can't fall out. Season the chicken with salt and pepper and brush with oil. Put a cup of water in a roasting dish with the chicken and roast in the oven at 180°C for approximately 1½ hours or until the chicken is cooked through. During the roasting process turn the chicken occasionally and add water as required to stop it from burning, baste with the liquid frequently.

Stuffing:
4 slices of white toast bread
150g butter
1 onion
150g mushrooms
2 eggs
¼ cup flour
fresh thyme
parsley
salt
pepper
nutmeg

Dice the toast bread into cubes and sauté in half the butter until lightly golden. Set aside in a large bowl and place a lid on top to keep the bread warm. With the remaining butter sauté the finely diced onions, add the sliced mushrooms and cook for 2–3 minutes then add to the bread. Add the finely chopped parsley and thyme, season with salt, nutmeg and white pepper. Whisk together the eggs and pour over. Gently mix together, replace the lid and leave for 10 minutes. Fold in the flour.

"Milk seems to take away the richness of the pork"
Mary Mathis

Milk Pork Loin

1 kg pork loin roast
1 tsp rock salt
1 tsp caraway seeds
3 cloves garlic
1 lemon rind
40ml olive oil
1 tbsp fresh thyme
½ tbsp sweet paprika
pepper
½ litre milk

Fill a large pot with approximately 1cm of water, and bring to the boil. Place the pork, skin down, in the boiling water for 4–5 minutes, then while warm and soft, scour the skin with a very sharp knife. Crush the salt, caraway seed, peeled and chopped garlic, chopped lemon rind, pepper, thyme and paprika in a mortar and pestle to a smooth paste. Add the olive oil and rub the paste into the pork loin. Rest for an hour.

In a roasting dish, just big enough to fit the pork in, pour in the milk, place the pork on top of it and slow roast in the oven at 170°C for 1–1½ hours or until cooked through.

Beef'n'Beer Hotpot

1 kg lean gravy beef
salt
pepper
2 tbsp Worcester sauce
2 tbsp flour
oil
2 cups small button mushrooms
2 cloves garlic
1 kg onions
2 tbsp tomato paste
2 tbsp malt vinegar
½ ltr beef stock
2 bottles ale
250g carrots
250g celery or celeriac
500g potatoes
4 sprigs fresh thyme
2 sprigs fresh rosemary

Season cubed beef with salt, pepper and Worcester sauce. Lightly dust with flour. Brown the meat in small batches in a very hot pan, turning to sear all sides. Remove each batch once browned. Once all the meat has been removed from the pan, add the chopped onions and garlic. Cook until golden. Add tomato paste and sauté for 3–4 minutes. De-glaze with vinegar. Add meat, beef stock and beer. Cover and simmer over a low heat (a crock-pot is ideal), until the meat is just tender—approximately 1 hour.

Add cubed vegetables and whole mushrooms, rosemary and thyme. Simmer until vegetables are cooked. Thicken with cornflour if necessary.

"Winter is the time of comfort, for good food and warmth..."
Anonymous

Gluehwein – Mulled wine

Gluehwein is the German/Austrian winter drink better—known here as mulled wine. Traditionally drunk after coming in from the snow, it is supposed to make you glow with warmth again. Drink this wine warm on a cold winter's evening, however be careful, the alcohol can go to your head quickly. Drink only when your really have come in from the cold and don't have to go out again!

1 bottle burgundy
2 cups water
peel of 1 lemon
whole cinnamon stick
3 whole cloves
⅓ cup sugar

Mix everything together in a saucepan and heat—do not boil, boiling will cause the alcohol to evaporate. Adjust the sugar to your liking.

Traditionally made with red wine, gluehwein is also enjoyable when made using dry white wine.

Braised Lamb Shanks

6 lamb shanks
salt
pepper
oil
2 onions
2 carrots
2 parsnips
3 tbsp tomato paste
2 bay leaves
300ml red wine
3 tbsp balsamic vinegar
1 ltr chicken stock
3 cloves garlic
1 lemon
parsley to garnish

Season the meat with salt and pepper, then brown in piping hot oil. Once browned remove from pan. Sauté diced onions until dark golden. Add diced carrot, parsnip and tomato paste. Sauté for a further 5 minutes. De-glaze with balsamic vinegar and red wine. Add chicken stock, bay leaves and meat. Cover and cook for a further 2–3 hours, until meat is tender.

Very finely chop lemon rind and garlic, and add to meat approximately 15 minutes before it is ready to be served. Serve on a bed of mashed potato or creamed polenta. Garnish with chopped parsley.

Lamb Navarin

1 kg boneless lamb shoulder
salt and pepper
flour
3 tbsp oil
2 cloves garlic
3 onions
1 tbsp tomato paste
100 ml red wine
1 can chopped tomatoes
1 ltr vegetable stock
1 bay leaf
sprig fresh marjoram
100g carrots
100g parsnips
200g potatoes

Cube lamb into 2–3cm pieces, season with salt and pepper, dust with flour and brown in a pan of hot oil. Remove the meat from the pan and set aside. Sauté the diced onions and garlic until golden, add tomato paste and stir. Add the red wine, tomatoes and stock. Add bay leaf and marjoram, and bring to the boil. Add the meat and simmer slowly for approximately one hour. Add the diced vegetables and simmer for a further 15 minutes or until everything is tender.

Adjust the seasoning before serving.

Recipe Index

Photo Index

Picnic at Hamurana Springs, 77
North Island's largest fresh water spring feeds into Lake Rotorua.

BMX rider, 82
Young local talent, Hamish Mcleod shows some fancy jumps.

Rainbow over Lake Rotorua with Mokoia Island 84/85

Seagulls at the Rotorua lake front, 86/87

Yellow dinghy, Lake Tarawera, 90
Trout sign on the city storm water drains, 90

Garden setting Paradise Valley, 93

Pohutu Geyser, 94/95
The largest geyser in the Te Whakarewarewa Thermal Valley, erupting up to 30 metres in the air several times a day.

Ohinemutu community gardens, 98
Denise La Grouw and the children from Rotorua Primary School, work in the Ohinemutu community gardens.

St Faiths Anglican Church, 100/101
On the edge of Lake Rotorua at Ohinemutu.

Autumn leaves, 102/103

Kuirau Park, 110
A public park endowed by Ngati Whakaue in the late 19th century, now a permanent recreation reserve. Rotorua streets are lined with maple trees, young lady baths her feet in the foot baths of Kuirau Park.

Tunohopu Marae, Ohinemutu, 112/113
Iri Te Kowai and her helpers catering in the kitchen on the marae. Food is cooked in modern steam boxes heated by geothermal.

Ohinemutu Village, 114
St Faith's Church in the early morning steam.

Rotorua Marathon, 117
In April/May each year the city hosts the Rotorua Marathon, with over 4,000 participants from around New Zealand and overseas competing on the course around Lake Rotorua.

Lake Rotorua at sunrise, 118/119
A single rower training on Lake Rotorua with Mokoia Island in the background.

Lake Rotorua on a still autumn morning, 121

Old house, Tarawera Road, 124
Mamaku drovers hut, 125

Hunt, 126/127
The hunt season is every winter, in New Zealand the hunt is for hare. These images were taken on a farm at Atiamuri.

Old Boat, Lake Rotoma, 129

Rainbow, Mt Ngongotaha, 135
This photo was taken in Paradise Valley.

Rural images, 137
Aerial topdressing, Ngakuru.
Jesus rock, Mamaku.
Autumn colours, Paradise Valley.
Dairy cows silhouette.
Woolshed, Sunnydowns Farm, Pukehangi Road.
Horses on farmland overlooking Lake Rotorua.

Autumn leaves, 138

Cat Eye Moonride, 140
An annual mountain bike event held in the Whakarewarewa Forest, hosting over 2,000 competitors.

Private jetty on Lake Tarawera, 142/143
Looking over to snow capped Mount Tarawera.

Pohutu Geyser, 144/145
The largest geyser in the Te Whakarewarewa Thermal Valley, erupting up to 30 metres in the air several times a day.

Rotorua Stadium, 146
The terrace seating at the stadium has been painted with a scene of the famous Pink and White Terraces which were destroyed by the eruption of Mt Tarawera in 1886.

Maori carving overlooking Lake Tarawera, 149

Acknowledgement

We would like to acknowledge and thank everybody who contributed in the making of this book, without you the book would not have been possible.

Disclaimer

The recipes in this book have been collected from various contributors in good faith and the publishers therefore accept no responsibility for any breach of copyright belonging to third parties. Not all recipes have been tested and, as such, the publishers are not liable for any inaccuracies in the recipes. The publishers have made every effort to ensure that the information in this book is complete and accurate.

Published in 2011 by Lasting Images, Rotorua
Copyright © photographs: Gerhard Egger, 2011
http://www.gerhardeggerphotographer.com
Food styling: Gerhard Egger
Production and editing: Gerhard and Henrietta Egger
Consultant editor: Shona Jennnings

ISBN: 978-0-473-20316-0

Prepress by Image Centre Ltd
Printed and bound in China by 1010 Printing

www.volcanickitchens.co.nz